Desegregating
America's Schools

Desegregating America's Schools

Larry W. Hughes
William M. Gordon
Larry W. Hillman

LONGMAN

New York and London

DESEGREGATING AMERICA'S SCHOOLS

Longman Inc., New York
Associated companies, branches, and
representatives throughout the world

Developmental Editor: Lane Akers
Editorial and Design Supervisor: Joan Matthews
Cover Design: Dan Serrano
Manufacturing and Production Supervisor: Robin B. Besofsky
Composition: Southern Graphic Arts, Inc.
Printing and binding: BookCrafters Inc.

Library of Congress Cataloging in Publication Data
Hughes, Larry W   1931–
    Desegregating America's schools.
    1. School integration–United States. 2. Discrimination in education–Law and
legislation–United States. I. Gordon, William MacGuire, 1935–   joint author.
II. Hillman, Larry, joint author. III. Title.
LC214.2.H83   370.19′342   79-28575

Manufactured in the United States of America

10 9 8 7 6 5 4 3 2 1

To Gordon Foster, who taught
us all.

Contents

List of Tables

List of Figures

Preface

Since 1954, with the historic declaration that separate could not be equal, educators, school board members, and jurists have agonized over the problem of educational equity. During the past quarter-century, the courts and school districts have attempted, often in a hesitating manner, to remove the elements of *de jure* segregation of schoolchildren by race and ethnic derivation.

More than vestiges remain of this monumental task, however. Court calendars throughout the land continue to have desegregation suits and countersuits on the docket. Many issues have yet to achieve resolution or even definition, and many communities have yet to face the problem adequately.

With the series of significant court cases that began with *Brown*,[1] and progressed through *Swann*,[2] *Keyes*,[3] *Milliken*,[4] and *Brinkman*,[5] to name a few, definition has been sought—at times achieved—and limitations imposed. One thing is certain: a public school system may not elect to maintain a dual school system, and a current school board may not continue discriminatory practices instituted by previous boards. With *Brown* as a base, buttressed by subsequent court decisions and such federal legislation as the Civil Rights Act of 1964, many American school districts are required to "do something."

This book aims to help those citizens and professionals faced with the task of doing something. It is a handbook for the development of a good desegregation plan. Although the suggestions and procedures rest on firm philosophic and legal bases, the book is dedicated to action.

The book comprises three sections plus appendixes. The first section, Chapters 1–3, examines the legal history and important issues to consider in plan development. Chapter 3 explains how to read a court order. This section provides the necessary knowledge base as well as a perspective for the development of a sound plan.

In the second section, Chapters 4–9, each chapter focuses directly on an aspect of plan development. Some of the areas examined are the kinds of data needed, techniques in the assignment of pupils and staff, ways to redraw attendance boundaries, the development of transportation routes, and the estimation of costs.

The final section, Chapters 10–11, discusses what happens after the plan is accepted. Chapter 10 provides insights into implementation procedures. Chapter 11 describes the "second-generation" problems that can be anticipated.

The appendixes, consisting of a glossary of terms and an annotated list of significant cases and events, provide supplementary information to the planner.

In short, this book is designed to assist the reader in understanding the nature of school segregation and to provide an understanding of the tools and techniques needed to desegregate schools. We hope that the book will serve as a rich resource for school administrators and administrators-in-training, boards of education, attorneys, and all who are interested in effectively addressing the issues of desegregation and educational equity.

Larry W. Hughes
William M. Gordon
Larry W. Hillman

NOTES

1. *Brown* v. *Board of Education of Topeka,* 347 U.S. 483 (1954).

2. *Swann* v. *Charlotte-Mecklinburg Board of Education,* 402 U.S. 1 (1971).

3. *Keyes* v. *School District No. 1, Denver, Colorado,* 93 S. Ct. 2686 (1973).

4. *Milliken* v. *Bradley,* 418 U.S. 717 (1974).

5. *Brinkman* v. *Dayton Board of Education,* 97 S.Ct. 2766 (1977).

Acknowledgments

Many persons have contributed to the development of this book. Colleagues, friends, students, and members of the education and legal profession have, over the years, through their interactions with the authors, provided thoughtful and thought-provoking substance. Sometimes these interactions were rancorous, in court and out, in closed sessions and open; more frequently, they were characterized by cordiality and earnest efforts to achieve consensus. In both instances the authors profited from the experience.

Five persons were especially helpful as the book moved from a series of random observations and narrative descriptions of shared experiences to a formally organized manuscript. Special thanks are due to Kathy Fritz for her tireless library research and manuscript reviews, to Doris Dunn and Barbara Greer for their excellence in the secretarial arts, and to Lloyd A. Williams and Frederick P. Venditti, for their counsel, advice, and insights.

1

School Desegregation in America: A Historical and Legal Framework

Henceforth, the defendants are under an affirmative obligation to reverse the consequences of their unconstitutional conduct. . . . This means that a preference not to bus, or for neighborhood schools, or in any other policy preference, can be validly maintained only if it will not interfere with the defendants' constitutional duty to desegregate. . . . Busing, the pairing of schools, redistricting with both contiguous and non-contiguous boundary lines, involuntary student and faculty assignments, and all other means, some of which may be distasteful to both school officials and teachers and parents, must be evaluated.[1]

So said the federal court in a Boston school desegregation case. The plaintiffs had contended that the school board intentionally brought about and maintained racial segregation in the Boston schools by such varied actions as pupil-assignment policies, manipulation of attendance zones to reflect segregated neighborhood residential patterns, the establishment of segregative grade structures and feeder patterns, and segregative school construction practices. The result, plaintiffs claimed, denied black schoolchildren equal protection of the laws and thus violated the Fourteenth Amendment to the U.S. Constitution. The court agreed, saying that all possible remedies to the situation must be "evaluated," no matter how initially "distasteful," any specific remedy might be to any particular patron or employee.

Since the historic *Brown* case in 1954,[2] millions of dollars of public money have been spent by school boards in desegregation litigation, frequently in ill-advised attempts to avoid the inevitable. Yet, important legal questions remain. How far must desegregation go; how far *can* it go? When must school districts participate in the desegregation of a neighboring district? When does the remedy exceed the degree of culpability?[3] How many racially identifiable schools can remain in a district before it ceases to be desegregated? What consideration must be given to the negative impact of economic segregation? Should staff desegregation include classified personnel such as custodians, cooks, and clerks? To what degree, if any, are private schools affected by the laws of desegregation[4] or in the overall desegregation plan of a district? Finally, there is that question frequently asked by both plaintiff and defendant and by desegregation plan developers and school attorneys: "What did the judge mean by that?" These and other questions are basic to current concerns about the development of good desegregation plans.

For several years, except among the most naive or retrogressive, the issue has not been whether schools must be desegregated. They must; of that there is no question. The text of *Brown* v. *Board of Education* need not be restated here. The latter-day questions are *how?* and *how much? how far?* and *who else?* and *what else?* and *who pays?*

HISTORICAL OVERVIEW

In the middle and late 1940s, the minorities in America, particularly blacks, seemed to reach a new level of consciousness. This consciousness took on the form of a quiet militancy, initially passive, that would not erupt into conflict on the streets until the 1960s. This militancy was conspicuously displayed in the nation's courtrooms as well-trained lawyers, blacks and whites, argued the cause of equal rights and freedom for all. Of course, earlier in our history blacks fought for certain rights in a number of cases. Nevertheless, not until the 1940s did demands on the courts and the larger society become great. A major reason for this was the assertive posture assumed by the National Association for the Advancement of Colored People. The NAACP, founded in New York City in 1909, began in the 1940s to put up large sums of money to fight for the "black cause" in the courts.

This surge of legal activity set the stage for a monumental decision in 1954. In 1953–54 the U.S. Supreme Court was asked to decide on five similar cases related to equal rights for all children who attended public schools. The principles raised related to

1. The legality, in the light of the Fourteenth Amendment of the U.S. Constitution, to deny equal education opportunity to any student

2. The possibility of giving people an equal educational opportunity if they were required by law to be separated according to their skin color

3. The constitutionality under the Fourteenth Amendment, therefore, of any state law which establishes separate school systems for whites and students of other skin colors

The Court decided to hear a sixth case, which was most representative of the five before it, and heard *Brown* v. *Board of Education of Topeka, Kansas.* In 1954, under Chief Justice Earl Warren, the U.S. Supreme Court handed down the *Brown* decision, which basically established that

1. The Fourteenth Amendment was intended to provide equal protection and therefore equal educational opportunity for all regardless of race or skin color.

2. It was not possible to provide that equal educational opportunity in schools or school systems which separated students on the basis of their race or skin color. It also stated that separate or segregated schools would deprive all students, regardless of race or skin color, of an equal educational opportunity.

3. A higher-level court can group a number of similar cases together and therefore the ruling on one would relate to all others.

In 1955 the Supreme Court spoke to *Brown* v. *Board* again. The Court established that states with laws maintaining segregated schools were in violation of the U.S. Constitution and that these laws must be struck from the code and the *de jure* segregation caused must be stopped as soon as possible.

This decision was the beginning of the desegregation activity in the United States. It reversed the *Plessy* "separate and equal decision" of 1896. The type of segregation it spoke to was *de jure* or segregation by law within one school district. The court also left the loophole of "all deliberate speed" or the "as soon as possible" interpretation. In most cases the laws pertaining to segregation in the south were dropped but little initiative was shown to correct the existing segregation.

The NAACP continued to litigate these situations on a costly case by case basis and some measure of progress was made. However, it was not until 1964, when the U.S. Congress passed the Civil Rights Act, that sufficient momentum was given to insure progress in implementing the court's ruling of 1954–55. The Civil Rights Act made it unlawful to operate the *de jure* segregated school system and stipulated penalties which could be levied upon the people and school districts violating these laws. Individuals could be fined severely and put in prison. School districts were in a position to lose all aid from the federal government if they did not comply.

A time schedule was set forth for desegregation of all districts in violation. When districts did not meet the time schedule they were punished according to the penalities of the law. *De jure* segregation began to vanish at a much more rapid pace.

LEGAL BASES

In their insistence upon the establishment of a single, racially integrated (unitary) school system for each community, the courts and the educational agencies of the federal government have established a reasonably consistent pattern since 1954. The 1954 *Brown* decision[5] rejected the doctrine of "separate but equal" set for schools in 1849[6] and reinforced by *Plessy* in 1896.[7] After the first *Brown* decision, *Bolling* v. *Sharpe* in Washington, D.C., applied desegregation orders to federally controlled schools with the charge that "Major responsibility for desegregating schools belongs to local school boards."[8] In the second *Brown* decision (1955), the Court clarified the roles of both courts and local school authorities in achieving school desegregation "with all deliberate speed."

... full implementation of these constitutional principles may require solution of various local school problems. School authorities have the primary responsibility for elucidating, assessing, and solving the problem. The action of school authorities constitutes good faith implementation of the governing constitutional principles.[9]

The net effect of these court decisions was to make *de jure* separation of the races in school illegal and to fix the responsibility for desegregation on local school authorities. In the years after the 1954 *Brown* decision, many court decisions have dealt with the details of segregation, but the basic position has not varied. Subsequent decisions have been legislatively reinforced by the Civil Rights Act of 1964, which made it unlawful to discriminate by race, creed, sex, or national origin.[10]

Current Federal Guidelines

Two important guidelines of the act are: (1) an observer should not be able to look at a school and identify it by the race for which it is intended; and (2) any board of education has an affirmative duty to desegregate the full school program, not just to cease discrimination. These guidelines have been used extensively in federal court decisions and by most federal agencies that finance school programs. In *Singleton*[11] the court, relying on the U.S. Office of Education statement of policy, took the position that "the later the start, the shorter the time allowed for transition."[12]

In 1967 the Fifth Circuit Court of Appeals relying on the USOE guidelines, stated: "School authorities have an affirmative duty to integrate faculties as well as facilities; . . . school desegregation . . . cannot be accomplished [merely] by a statement of policy." The court further stated that "racial composition of faculty in a school should not vary more than ten percent from the racial composition of all the teachers in the system."[13]

In *Swann*[14] the Supreme Court decided that the mandates of the *Brown* decisions must be implemented by local districts via any available means. *Swann* not only reaffirms the unconstitutionality of the separate-but-equal doctrine but clarifies what school districts must do to eliminate all vestiges of a dual school system: "We hold that the pairing and grouping of noncontiguous school zones is a permissible tool and such action is to be considered in light of the objectives sought." With regard to transportation, the Court said: "We find no basis for holding that the local school authorities may not be required to employ bus transportation as one tool of school desegregation. Desegregation plans cannot be limited to the walk-in school." In effect, *Swann* stated that any administrative devices used to operate the previous school program should be used to accomplish a unitary school system, even though the implementation may look bizarre.

Keyes[15] extended *Swann*. In the early spring of 1969, the Denver school board adopted three resolutions designed to desegregate schools in the predominantly black Park Hill area of the city. After a local election resulted in a board majority opposed to the three integration resolutions, the plan was scrapped. At that point, black plaintiffs filed suit. Initially the plaintiffs in *Keyes* sought a limited goal; they sued only to desegregate schools in Park Hill. Achieving success in that endeavor, they expanded their suit to secure desegregation of all schools in the Denver school district. The Supreme Court determined that since the new school board "backtracked," the board was now guilty of *de jure* segregation because they were acting to deny rights provided under the U.S. Constitution.[16] In *Keyes* the Court specifically said:

1. "... we have held that where plaintiffs proved that a current condition of segregated schooling exists within a school district where a dual system was compelled or authorized by statute at the time of our decision in *Brown* v. *Board,* the state automatically assumes an affirmative duty "to effectuate a transition to racially nondiscriminatory school system," that is, to eliminate from the public schools within their school system "all vestiges of state-imposed segregation." [*Swann* v. *Charlotte-Mecklenburg Board of Education.*]

2. "... we hold that a finding of intentionally segregative school board actions in a meaningful portion of a school system, as in this case, creates a presumption that other segregated schooling within the system is not adventitious."

3. "It is enough that we hold that the mere assertion of such policy is not dispositive where, as in this case, the school authorities have been found to have practiced *de jure* segregation in a meaningful portion of the school system by techniques that indicated that the "neighborhood school" concept has not been maintained free of manipulation."

Involving Other Districts

An important new issue has arisen in the last few years and has to do with neighboring districts participating in the desegregation of a district. In Richmond, Virginia, a case related to the crossing of school district boundaries to achieve desegregation.[17] This was the first indication that the courts were beginning to consider a metropolitan remedy. They seemed to be questioning the rationality of desegregating within one school district's boundary. Another prominent case of this kind was *Milliken* v. *Bradley.*[18] A federal court found both Detroit and the Michigan State Board of Education guilty of maintaining a segregated school district. In the process of considering a remedy the court joined the surrounding suburban school districts in the case and directed that a metropolitan plan be developed. Several plans were developed and were presented before the court. The surrounding districts challenged this approach and pleaded the metropolitan issue before the U.S. Supreme Court. The decision of the Court basically maintained the integrity of the school district as a political subdivision. The Court established that each school district would have to be proven guilty of contributing to the segregation of the Detroit school district before it could be included in a metropolitan plan.

Other metropolitan remedies have been found legal, however. In Louisville–Jefferson County, Kentucky, a metropolitan result was achieved through a 1975 merger made possible under state law. The result extended the desegregation of Louisville schools to all of Jefferson County. In Wilmington, Delaware, a metropolitan remedy was requested when it was shown that the county that surrounded Wilmington in fact contributed to the segregation of Wilmington public schools.[19] One court-ordered plan was to examine a metropolitan remedy. The issue of a metropolitan desegregation remedy is not resolved, but, despite *Milliken* and because of *Wilmington,* federal judges continue to look to suburban school districts as a possible source of help. In the summer of 1978 U.S. District Judge Finis Cowan directed the Houston Independent School District to investigate whether the predominantly white suburban school districts would help Houston desegregate its schools in some sort of voluntary cooperative program.[20] The issue of metropolitan remedies remains unclarified. Even in *Wilmington,* the court merely asked that one such plan be proposed; it has not yet acted on its acceptability.

Desegregating the schools of a school district is not an easy task even when it is undertaken voluntarily. When it occurs as a result of a court order, after months of litigation, it frequently is even more difficult because of incipient acrimony. The legal bases are at once clear (e.g., There shall be no *de jure* desegregation) and unclear (e.g., How much is enough? When is *de facto* a product of earlier *de jure* actions by school boards, or administrators?) Moreover, we have seldom worked with school boards and school administrators in desegregation cases where these people did not feel deeply that their situation was "different" and that the court simply "didn't understand." Thus, litigation continues, as does segregation.

One of the larger problems confronting and confounding public schools in a desegregation process is the dollar cost. When a board of education, by court order or voluntarily, chooses to desegregate, the responsibility for paying for the desegregation is most frequently left to the local board and local taxpayers. Recently, state boards of education, and thus the entire state, have been made party to the suits, and court orders have directed them to pay part of the cost.[21] For the most part, however, the burden of paying for desegregation has remained at the local level. In many instances the cost has been enormous, including legal fees, planning, staffing, materials, administration, and purchases of new vehicles, plus the storage, maintenance, and security of those vehicles. In some cases the cost has also included construction of new educational facilities and training programs for people so they might function properly in the new environment. The federally funded Emergency School Assistance Act has made it possible for school districts to secure some money for the training of staff and the delivery of special programs to some students in newly desegregated situations.

Some districts have spent so much money in litigation, as well as in implementation of desegregation, that the expense has substantially contributed to a deficit financial condition. Cleveland, Ohio, and Jefferson County, Kentucky, are examples of this. Frequently, too, when plans are imposed on local school districts by the courts, local taxpayers are reluctant to support requests for additional tax money.[22] State legislatures have maintained a posture similar to the federal government in relation to funding. They have refrained from making general tax monies available to pay for desegregation costs.

When making plans or projecting the future, it is important to study the mood of the courts. A plan that may have been acceptable at one time may be frowned upon by the courts at another time. Where courts today seem to be looking favorably upon the establishment of magnet schools as an alternative approach to desegregation, it was only a short time ago that the same courts would not accept plans suggesting magnets. At present, the Supreme Court is sending mixed signals. In *Brinkman* the Court agreed that the remedy applied in the Dayton, Ohio, plan was too expensive and went beyond what was needed.[23] This reopened questions of "enough or too much." The Court has also allowed Columbus, Ohio,[24] to delay the implementation of a fully developed plan for at least one year. Such signals are not clear and must be studied carefully.[25]

What about certain residual effects of an implemented plan on an anticipated desegregation procedure? Again, it is difficult to predict "what will happen if," and the courts have not been particularly interested in or persuaded by the presumed prescience of either plaintiffs or defendants. Such phenomena as "white flight" and second-generation desegregation difficulties, while frequently a matter of testimony, are often not addressed directly by either the court or the desegregation plan.[26]

Desegregation plans are "body mixers" pure and simple. Nevertheless, planners are careful to consider the probable immediate and long-range impact of plan implementation and try to draw a plan in such a way that negative effects are mitigated. Developing a fair plan—one that meets both the intent and the spirit of the law—is a difficult task, all the more so because of a continuing lack of clarity issuing from case law. Consider the words of Hooker:

> The safest prediction about the future is that school desegregation will continue. Many issues remain unresolved. Second generation problems such as within-school segregation will emerge. Central to future litigation is the clarification of the meaning of the purpose or intent to segregate; the equal protection clause of the Fourteenth Amendment; the troublesome concepts *de facto* and *de jure* segregation. With the tendency of the Court to fashion definitions out of whole cloth, we have a situation analogous to Humpty Dumpty's statement to Alice: "When I use a word, it means just what I choose it to mean—neither more nor less."[27]

SELECTED COURT DECISIONS

Brown v. *Board of Education of Topeka,* 347 U.S. 483, 493 (1954).

Brown v. *Board of Education of Topeka,* 75 S.Ct. 753, 349 U.S. 294, 99 L.Ed. 1083 (1955).

Dayton Board of Education v. *Brinkman,* 97 S.Ct. 2766 (1977).

Dayton Board of Education v. *Brinkman*, 99 S. Ct. 2766 (1977).

Evans v. *Buchanan*, 555 F.2d 373 (C.A. Del. 1977).

Goss v. *Board of Education*, 373 U.S. 683, 83 S.Ct. 1405, 10 L.Ed.2d 632 (1963).

Keyes v. *School District No. 1, Denver, Col.*, 521 F.2d. 465, Cert. Denied; *Congress of Hispanic Educators* v. *School District No. 1., Denver, Col.*, 96 S.Ct. 806, two cases, 423 U.S. 1066, 46 L.Ed. 2d 657 (C.A. Col. 1975).

Milliken v. *Bradley*, 97 S.Ct. 2749 (U.S. Mich. 1977).

Plessy v. *Ferguson*, 163 U.S. 537, 16 S.Ct. 1138, 41 L.Ed. 256 (1896).

Singleton v. *Jackson Municipal Separate School District*, 419 F2d 1211.

Swann v. *Charlotte-Mecklenburg Board of Education*, 402 U.S. 1 (1971)

Taylor v. *Board of Education of City School District of New Rochelle*, 294 U.S. 940, 82 S.Ct. 382, 7 L.Ed.2d 339 (1961).

SELECTED BIBLIOGRAPHY

Coleman James S. "Racial Segregation in the Schools: New Research with New Policy Implications," *Phi Delta Kappan* 57, no. 2 (October 1975): 75.

Fishel, Leslie H., Jr., and Benjamin Quarles, *The Black American: A Documentary History*. Chicago, Ill.: Scott, Foresman, 1970. 549 pages.

Foster, Gordon. "Desegregating Urban Schools: A Review of Techniques." *Harvard Educational Review* 43, no. 1 (February 1973): 5–36.

Gordon, William M., and Robert J. Simpson. "School Desegregation—Is Busing for U.S.?" *Nolpe School Law Journal*, Spring 1973, 27–36.

Hooker, Clifford P., ed. *The Courts and Education, The Seventy-Seventh Yearbook of the National Society for the Study of Education*. Chicago: The National Society, 1978. See especially chapters 4 and 13.

Hughes, Larry W. *Informal and Formal Community Forces: External Influences on Schools and Teachers*, Morristown, N.J.: General Learning Press, 1976.

Levine, Daniel U., and Robert J. Havighurst. *The Future of Big-City Schools*. Berkeley, Calif.: McCutchan, 1977. 283 pages.

McDonald, Laughlin. *Racial Equality*. Skokie, Ill.: National Textbook, 1977. 147 pages.

Myrdal, Gunnar. *An American Dilemma.* New York: Harper & Row, 1944.

Nevas, Susan R. "Factors in Desegregation and Integration." *Equal Opportunity Review*, Institute for Urban and Minority Education, Teachers College, Columbia University, Fall 1977.

NOTES

1. *Morgan* v. *Hennigan*, 379 F. Supp. 410 (1974). For a case involving Mexican Americans, where a similar remedy was prescribed, see *Cisneros* v. *Corpus Christi Independent School District*, 467 F.2d 142 (1972).

2. *Brown* v. *Board of Education of Topeka*, 347 U.S. 483 (1954).

3. See *Brinkman* v. *Dayton Board of Education,* 97 S.Ct. 2766, on remand *Brinkman* v. *Gilligan,* 561 F.2d 652 (U.S. Ohio 1977), for an examination of this issue.

4. For example, see *Gonzales* v. *Fairfax-Brewster School, Inc.,* 363 F.Supp. 1200 (1973) wherein the court issued a permanent injunction to prohibit a private school from using race as an admissions criterion and awarded pecuniary damages to the plaintiffs for their "embarrassment, humiliation and mental anguish."

5. *Brown* v. *Board of Education of Topeka* (1954).

6. *Roberts* v. *City of Boston,* 5 Cush. 198 (1849).

7. *Plessy* v. *Ferguson, Error to the Supreme Court of the State of Louisiana,* 163, U.S. 537, 16 S.Ct. 1138 (1896).

8. *Brown,* v. *Board of Education of Topeka,* 349 U.S. 294, 299 (1955). *Bolling* v. *Sharpe,* 347 U.S. 497, 74 S.Ct. 693 (1954). This case is interesting since it came from the District of Columbia and therefore was based upon the Fifth Amendment (due process) as contrasted with *Brown,* which used the Fourteenth Amendment.

9. *Brown,* v. *Board of Education of Topeka.* (1955).

10. *General Statement of Policies Under Title VI of the Civil Rights Act of 1964 Respecting Desegregation of Elementary and Secondary Schools* (federal document, U.S. Government Printing Office, April 1965). Title VI of this act deals specifically with the desegregation of elementary and secondary schools. In 1965 the U.S. Office of Education issued guidelines that have had a great effect on the desegregation of school districts, especially where funding is involved.

11. *Singleton* v. *Jackson Municipal Separate School District,* 348 F.2d 729, 731 (1965). A combination of 16 Fifth Circuit cases.

12. Ibid. See also *Alexander* v. *Holmes County Board of Education,* U.S., 90 S.Ct. 29, which supervened and supported *Singleton.*

13. Samuel B. Etheridge, "Court Decisions: Impact of Staff Balance," *Educational Leadership,* December 1968, pp. 235–239, citing *U.S.* v. *Jefferson Board of Education,* 380 F.2d 385 U.S. 840 (1967).

14. *Swann* v. *Charlotte-Mecklenburg Board of Education,* 402 U.S. 1, (1971). See also *Morgan* v. *Henningan,* 379 F.Supp. 410 (1974).

15. *Keyes* v. *School District No. 2., Denver, Colorado,* 93 St. 2686 (1973).

16. Therefore, the establishment that a school district was *de facto* segregated may put a board on notice that they should look for a way to improve the situation. If a public board of education continues to operate a known or established *de facto* segregated school system they can be found to be practicing *de jure* segregation. The Court did make a sharp *de jure* desegregation however and thereby seemed to affirm that while *de jure* was clearly unconstitutional, *de facto* was beyond the Court's purview.

17. *Bradley* v. *School Board, City of Richmond, Virginia,* 416 U.S. 696 (1974).

18. *Milliken* v. *Bradley,* 418 U.S. 717 (1974). See also *U.S.* v. *Board of School Commissioners, Indianapolis,* 419 F.Supp. 180 (1975), appealed.

19. *Evans* v. *Buchanon,* 555 F.2d. 373 (C.A. Del. 1977). For the Kentucky situation, see *Newburg Area Council* v. *Board of Education,* 510 F.2d 1358 (1974).

20. The answer from the suburbs—No! (See the December 5, 1978, *Houston Chronicle.*)

21. For example: *Penick* v. *Columbus Board of Education,* 429 F.Supp. 229 (D.C. Ohio 1977) and *Reed* v. *Rhodes,* 422 F.Supp. 708 (N.D. Ohio 1976).

22. Whether the taxpayers' resistance is because of the plan or is simply a manifestation of the current "taxpayers' revolt" in all aspects of publicly funded endeavors is uncertain, however.

23. *Brinkman* v. *Dayton Board of Education,* 97 S.Ct. 2766, on remand, *Brinkman* v. *Gilligan,* 561 F.2d 652 (U.S. Ohio 1977).

24. *Penick* v. *Columbus Board of Education,* 429 F.Supp. 229 (D.C. Ohio 1977).

25. Other signals: *Pasadena (Pasadena* v. *Spangler,* 44 U.S.L.W. 5117) in 1976, limiting the period of federal court jurisdiction; and *Austin (Austin Independent School District* v. *U.S.,* 44 U.S.L.W. 3413), also in 1976, restricting the use of busing as a remedy.

26. The issue of "white flight" has been a matter of court attention as it relates to resegregation and the responsibility of school boards. In general, school boards have not been held responsible for any subsequent resegregation. The court spoke to this first in *Swann* when it indicated that boards were not constitutionally required to make year-by-year adjustments in response to population mobility. Later, an even more definitive statement was made in *Pasadena* v. *Spangler.*

27. Clifford Hooker, "Issues in School Desegregation Litigation," Chapter IV in Hooker (ed.), *The Courts and Education,* Seventy-seventh yearbook of the National Society for the Study of Education, Chicago: *The Society,* 1978, p. 115.

2

Social, Political, and Educational Issues

When it becomes apparent that a large proportion of the schools in the community are mostly attended by students of one race or ethnic group, and something must be done to change this, several social, political and educational issues arise. Most, if not all, of these issues are matters of concern in desegregation plan development, although some issues often confound rather than clarify thinking. The issues that seem to cause controversy and need better definition are

- The difference between *desegregation* and *integration*
- The impact of intellectual and economic segregation
- The observed tendency of groups to engage in out-migration from the city
- How to cope with population declines and imminent school closings
- Involuntary transportation of students
- Volunteerism, freedom of choice, and magnet schools as desegregation techniques
- Educational parks, extended neighborhoods, and metropolitanism as desegregation techniques

These issues have a confounding quality because they are manifested in different ways in different communities and because some lack precise definition. As aspects of firm proposals, or even as matters for conversation, each frequently has an inflammatory quality.

This chapter describes and defines the issues so that planners, school personnel, and community members can more readily analyze desegregation proposals and select options that give promise of success unencumbered by sloganeering, catch phrases, and glibness.

DESEGREGATION-INTEGRATION: A DISTINCTION

Newspapers and politicians seemingly are determined to use the terms *desegregation* and *integration* synonomously. The terms are not synonomous. They relate to each other but have different meanings. In *Brown* v. *Board of Education*[1] some of the compelling arguments centered on multiracial interaction in desegregated situations, but the Court only spoke within its jurisdiction to break down any and all governmental barriers that deprived citizens of their Fourteenth Amendment rights. Thus, the Court ordered that public schools be desegregated, that is, to proceed in "the physical mixing of races without regard to relative statuses of the two groups."[2] In other words, districts were ordered to establish an arrangement whereby white students would be placed in schools that were predominantly black, and black children would be put in schools that were predominantly white. (*Balance* was not an early issue; later it was defined to mean a racial mix that would represent the racial mix of the district.)

Desegregation can, and in many instances does, become a mechanical process. Some years ago, one of the authors participated in a situation where a superintendent of a county school district in the South met with consultants in his office and within two hours drew up a plan to desegregate his district. This emphasizes the dispatch with which one can comply with a court mandate. But would such a mechanistic approach provide broad commitment to this plan? Would there be changed behavior on the part of the teachers? Would there be some element of acceptance that would or could lead to changed human relationships? The answer is most likely no. These questions relate not to body mixing but to integration. Nevertheless, the superintendent's activity complied with the Court mandate of 1954, even though the Court might have been thinking of something broader.

Many social scientists have insisted that the Court was thinking of integration as its ultimate goal, and that argument seems logical when one considers the arguments of *Brown.* Integration, however, cannot be mandated by courts because it is a social process and not controlled by the state. The noted sociologist Kenneth Clark has referred to integration as a subjective, psychological attitudinal process that goes beyond desegregation.[3] Integration is the process of mutual acceptance of, and respect for, other races and includes some level of cultural assimilation between races. Most social scientists agree that integration cannot occur without racial interaction. Clark went so far as to point out that there could be no integration before desegregation because social change and determined behavioral change precede and often govern affective and attitudinal changes. He went on to indicate that, even though blacks have been the chief victims of gross injustices in the segregated system, white youngsters have much to gain because desegregation releases the white youngster from an isolated school situation that is unlike the realities of the future and contemporary world.[4]

Studies conducted by Weinberg,[5] Pettigrew,[6] Gordon,[7] and Forehand et al.[8] indicate that even though desegregation is working, there are few signs of integration. Levels of acceptance of desegregation vary as one looks from group to group. In places where plans were well drawn and were accepted by community and school personnel, integration is much farther along than in other districts.

Desegregation of public schools is the law in the United States. Courts can only enforce compliance with the law; courts cannot mandate integration. If the ultimate result of desegregation is to be integration, then it will be done through the extra-legal efforts of leaders in the school, the community, and the nation as a whole. Such an effort will require organized activities on the part of teachers, administrators, and community members. Chapters 10 and 11 in this volume offer some insights into this process.

ECONOMIC AND INTELLECTUAL SEGREGATION

The courts have consistently spoken to the mixing of races in schools to achieve desegregation and, in a great number of instances, this has been accomplished. The courts have implied integration but have realized that they were without authority to cause social integration and behavioral realignment to take place. Nevertheless, it can be observed that the most successful desegregation plans have been those in which social integration has been a goal, and great effort was made to achieve this. Because there is insufficient research in this subject area, it is much more difficult to evaluate than the more obvious facts and figures of sheer body mixing.

Other factors have a tendency to cloud the issues but have frequently been overlooked by the courts. These factors fall into a category of economic and intellectual isolation or segregation. People of means frequently separate themselves into communities or neighborhoods where people with like incomes live. It is possible to read the real estate billboards on the periphery of any large city and know at once what economic life style one is joining by purchasing a house in this or that subdivision.

In the economic makeup of a school population, school desegregators should be aware that matching low-income whites with low-income blacks might simply substitute one form of segregation for another. Generally, neighborhoods on the lower end of the economic ladder have the least amount of political leverage and the smallest voice in school matters. A desegregation planner should be aware of the economics of various neighborhoods and, wherever possible, avoid establishing schools that draw disproportionately from a single economic class. Balancing economic classes along with racial balancing has a tendency to create healthy school climates and address students' individual needs more efficiently.

In general, people of similar intellect also see fit to isolate themselves in conclaves. Intellectual development of course often links to money because of the cultural and professional opportunities afforded the well educated. But this is not necessarily the pattern; wealth and native intelligence do not always link. Intellectual "communities" might also be connected with a specific professional endeavor. People living in these intellectual villages exchange information and gain from the interaction. Some outstanding contributions to the development of society have come from established intellectual communities.

Intellectual segregation within schools generally takes place when schools that have been racially desegregated go to a system of academic tracking or ability grouping. The courts have been quick to speak to situations where tracking or ability grouping causes resegregation in the school. Black students who come from segregated school settings have a tendency to be less well developed educationally than their white counterparts. Thus, if a school system decides to group by ability, there is a high probability that the low-ability sections will be primarily minority students, and the higher sections will be primarily nonminority students. Resegregation on intellectual grounds is probably as damaging to students as desegregation on racial grounds. Much of the literature talks about the self-fulfilling prophecies that emanate because of teacher expectations and self-perceptions. These self-fulfilling prophecies can adversely affect learning and teaching and should be avoided wherever possible when desegregating a school system.

It seems that the intent of desegregation is to mix races with the idea that this was a basic dividing line in American society. Desegregation orders thereby focused on ethnic conclaves and their obvious segregation and ignored economic and intellectual conclaves. Great social value and a continuing fluid social structure may be obtained by providing a school setting that is cross-sectional economically, socially, and intellectually, as well as racially and ethnically. Such an environment can be maximally stimulative and positive. It does, however, greatly complicate the task of the desegregation planner.

The desegregation planner can do some things within the present law and guidelines. No law would keep one from conducting a demographic survey of the community and making decisions on racial mixes that would also recognize economic and intellectual orientations. If challenged about the pupil movement beyond that required for racial desegregation, a planner might not find it too difficult to convince the court of the need. This area is new, and the first tries have been hesitating and frustrating; but futuristic planners are aware of its importance. Certainly the educator can facilitate appropriate mixing and interaction within the school by avoiding rigid tracking schemes, developing enlightened counseling programs, and reducing the economic impact of participating in some extracurricular programs.

POPULATION DECLINE

Population trends have a tendency to be cyclical, and recent peaks and valleys in birthrates have been well documented. The 1930s, the decade of the Great Depression, saw a significant decline in the birthrate, followed by a great increase in births after the Second World War, and again a decline in the late 1960s and '70s. There is some indication that the 1980s will witness another upswing in population growth.

Enough data are available to establish the fact that the American family is getting smaller, the population is getting older, and birthrate and macro-population shifts in many parts of the country are causing the population to decline at an increasing rate. This decline, of course, is more noticeable in areas of concentrated population. Even if the decline were uniform, a 1 percent fall in the population of Chicago, for example, would result in a decline of approximately 60,000 people, where a 1 percent population decline in Oxford, Ohio, would be approximately 70 people. The impact of these two declines on schools, commerce, and the job market would be significantly different—one highly noticeable and the other negligible. But population declines are not uniform across the country in urban, suburban, and rural settings.

There has been a disproportionate drop in the populations of certain urban areas, especially in the North. Even in urban areas in the South and Southwest that are experiencing significant population gains, the city proper frequently experiences a population decline and the adjacent suburban areas are faced with uncontrolled growth.[9]

This decline in city population is generally disproportionately composed of the white population. Factors other than an overall decline in birth rate that tend to contribute to a population decline in urban areas are high instances of crime, the abandonment of the urban setting by certain businesses and industries, the declining reputation of the quality of the urban setting, and the allure of the "American dream" exemplified by suburban living. Though this list is general and not exhaustive, it contains major concerns for anyone charged with desegregating a school system.

A decline in urban enrollment means an excess of schoolrooms, a changing ethnic or racial ratio, a greater burden for the educational cost falling on a smaller population, and a general decline in the quality of life of the urban setting. This last, a decline in the quality of life of the urban setting, is exacerbated by the tendency of shopping areas, restaurants, theaters, professional people, and financial institutions to relocate in the suburbs. Thus the core of the city is left with abandoned buildings, less economically fortunate people, and few attractions that persuade the young to in-migrate.

Designers of school desegregation plans must examine these trends and attempt to project populations based on current records of decline. As stated earlier, the economically fortunate tend to out-migrate at a greater rate when faced with the prospects of school desegregation. Even though this may be predictable, it cannot become a reason to abandon attempts to provide equal access to an education for all children within the community.

HOW TO CLOSE A SCHOOL

Many urban communities, especially those in the North and East, are experiencing a significant decline in school populations. This decline is caused by lower birthrates and exacerbated by the out-migration from urban centers and macropopulation shifts to the South and Southwest. Regardless of the reasons for the reduction in population, the results are the same: an excess of school buildings in urban school districts.

This excess capacity can be both a blessing and curse to a school system. The blessing is that obsolete facilities can be taken out of service and, if done carefully, this can facilitate the desegregation of buildings left in service. The curse to the school system lies in the fact that, with the notion of the "neighborhood school," most citizens favor taking unused facilities out of service as long as it is not "their school." School administrators have the delicate task of closing unneeded facilities while at the same time keeping citizens from becoming agitated about the specific buildings taken out of service.

Chapter 6 provides criteria that can be used to determine which buildings should be taken out of service. The desegregation planner must exercise caution as to how decisions for school closings are presented to the public. A deceivingly appealing, although frequently misused, course of action in many communities has been the establishment of a citizens' "blue ribbon" committee charged to evaluate the existing school facilities and make a report to the school board. Often, when a citizen group gets involved in this kind of activity, it works long and hard, makes conscientious recommendations to the board, and then finds that its recommendations are not fully implemented. The end result is the opposite of what the board hoped to achieve. The board was hoping for a feeling of participation on the part of the community; in fact, it alienated a segment of the community because its citizens' efforts were not recognized. They were simply a sham committee put together to delude the community with a false notion of involvement.

This is not to say that citizen groups should not be involved in desegregation planning, nor does it say that citizen groups should not be involved in determining which buildings should be taken out of service. But groups composed primarily of nonprofessionals should be given specific guidelines and criteria to use in making their judgments and recommendations. Citizen group participation, when accomplished in a positive manner, can be most helpful in the development of desegregation plans.[10]

The closing of obsolete schools or schools that have enrollments far less than capacity can be beneficial to school desegregation. First, the judicious closing of buildings can cause neighboring schools to become desegregated through the reassignment of students. Second, the closing of schools with enrollments much lower than capacity is a cost saving for the school system. It must be kept in mind that the desegregation of a school system requires additional expenses, and these expenses may be at least partially offset by monies saved in taking underused facilities out of operation. Third, the closing of facilities allows the school system to consolidate existing programs and perhaps develop new programs or organizational configurations that were not possible when small student populations were spread over several facilities.

A school desegregation planner must approach the recommendation to remove certain facilities from service with some degree of caution. Schools frequently have an identity shared by community members. There could be considerable community upheaval if a closing was done indiscriminately and without the decision having been based on sensible and understood criteria.

VOLUNTEERISM AND FREEDOM OF CHOICE

When desegregation plans began being viewed by the public as an arbitrary reassignment of students for political or social reasons, communities began exercising pressure on local school boards. In an attempt to satisfy the political climate of the community, and also to satisfy court requirements for the elimination of racially identifiable schools, a series of voluntary, or freedom of choice, plans were developed. These plans were built around several formulas with the common feature of allowing the student to select a learning environment rather than be assigned arbitrarily.

Under this plan, school boards declared the school system to be without attendance boundaries and then allowed students to select whichever school they wanted to attend. The premise was that this was an exercise in democracy because it allowed for choice built on personal preference. The immediate effect of plans of this nature was to continue all-white and all-black schools within most school districts because few students selected schools other than the ones they were already attending.

The courts, addressing freedom of choice plans, have held that school systems must have some form of attendance boundaries for each school and that in order for a student to choose a school he or she is not assigned to, the choice must improve the racial balance of both the sending and receiving school. That is, if a student wishes to transfer from School A to School B, the departure from School A must improve the racial balance of that school by helping it achieve a balance more nearly like the current racial ratio of the district as a whole. Moreover, it must also improve the racial balance of School B by helping that school approach the racial balance of the community. In essence this means that for a student to transfer, the transfer must be from a school where his or her race is in the majority and into a school where the student's race is the minority. Only under these circumstances will the court allow freedom of choice to be an aspect of a desegregation plan.

A larger arena of volunteerism is developing in some communities involved in desegregation. Some school systems provide magnet schools, some school systems allow students from outside the school system to attend special programs inside the school system, and some school systems establish special-focus educational programs. These voluntary schools generally have the common feature of a unique program not found anywhere else in the system or a program that focuses on the educational needs of a select group of students. Historically, programs of this nature have not been highly successful as desegregative techniques. There is a tendency on the part of white middleclas students to shun any but a college preparatory program. And many black students view these programs as compensatory and patronizing instead of programs to fill legitimate educational needs within the community.

Though volunteerism and freedom of choice have a democratic ring to them, and appeal to the emotional needs of local citizens, they tend not to work, or if they work, they involve an insignificant portion of the total school population.[11]

MAGNET SCHOOLS

The notion that students should be arbitrarily assigned to a school in order to achieve a racial mix has been viewed by some segments of the population as a circumvention of their right to freedom of choice. This is an anomaly because, prior to school desegregation, little if any choice was given a parent in determining where a child would attend public school. Historically, children have been assigned to public school by virtue of where they lived and not by virtue of where they would like to attend. Consequently, a rallying point for many who strongly oppose school desegregation has been a desire to retain the "neighborhood school."

The neighborhood school epitomizes to many people the right of free choice and the components of a personalized education. These notions are fallacious; school assignment historically has had little to do with free choice, and the personalization of program has long been a characteristic of individual teachers rather than a function of the residential proximity of the student. This knowledge notwithstanding, terms such as "forced busing," "freedom of choice," and "neighborhood school" have become political slogans with little to do with education. A little remembered fact (except by courts and plaintiffs) is that schoolchildren in this country have historically been removed from their immediate home area when greater educational benefit was to be derived elsewhere (e.g., witness the consolidated rural school systems).

Desegregation planners, in an attempt to circumvent the inflamed feelings of many community residents, have tried to interject elements of freedom of choice in school assignment through a device commonly referred to as *magnet schools*. A magnet school, by definition, is a school with a unique educational program available to those students in the larger community who opt to participate in the learning experience. Thus, magnet schools with programs focusing on gifted students, vocational opportunities, science or math, fine arts, etc., have been developed as components of desegregation plans. Generally, these programs are housed in locations that are accessible to both black and white populations; they are programs equipped with special facilities, equipment, and materials, and are frequently staffed by selected teachers. Students are allowed to elect to participate in the magnet program or be assigned to a school by virtue of residence.

In school systems with programs of this nature, school officials can admit volunteer students who qualify for the program by applying criteria that specify a particular racial balance. The magnet school allows the desegregation process to take place through the mechanism of program option and thus reduces the arbitrary assignment of students to schools on the basis of race. Because it is based on excellence and particularity of program, all, it is argued, benefit from the magnet school. Unfortunately, magnet schools simply have not worked as a tool of desegregation.

Though this voluntary mechanism appeals to many educators and school boards, it has not proved effective in school desegregation. School systems in Dallas, Houston, Indianapolis, Minneapolis, and Philadelphia point to their magnet programs as important parts of their school desegregation plan; in fact, these programs have had minimal impact on the overall racial balances of these systems. Instances where magnet programs have been implemented reveal that the number of students voluntarily participating in the programs is small and in most cases represents relatively high investments in time and dollars for recruitment and transportation. Additionally, many magnet programs are little more than standard programs offered in a different setting to a small number of students whose parents want them in a desegregated school. Educational benefits from programs of this nature are negligible and costs are high, although for a few students, the social benefits may be great indeed.

Magnet schools suffer from several things. First, school systems generally initiate magnet programs only after they have been found guilty of official segregative acts. When the community is informed that this "unique, educationally exciting program" is offered to improve the quality of education, the citizens are astute enough to realize that the primary reason for offering the program is to racially mix the school system. The educational merit of the plan, if it is not suspect to the populace, is, at least in the minds of most, secondary. The understandable attitude on the part of the public is, "If magnet schools are so damned good in and of themselves, why haven't we been doing it all along?"

Second, as a general rule, white students will not opt for magnet programs if it means attending class in formerly all-black schools. Logic would dictate that if parents were motivated primarily by the quality of education their children were receiving, program location would make little difference. This is not the case.

Third, magnet programs are expensive to establish and maintain. Exemplary and special magnet schools cost more money than regular schools. This is not necessarily undesirable, but the fact that they cost more needs to be recognized; it may become a subject of great controversy.

Fourth, volunteerism is at best tenuous. Without backups or guarantees, most courts view magnet schools only as add-ons rather than as important components of a desegregation plan.

The magnet school has the appeal of allowing parents to select those programs most appropriate for their children's needs. This factor disarms the arguments of antibusing, antiforced choice, and neighborhood school groups. But as a practical matter, volunteerism in desegregation has not proved to be an effective desegregative tool, especially in large school systems. There are no instances where a major school system has noticeably desegregated its public schools by using a voluntary magnet program.

EXTENDED NEIGHBORHOODS
AND EDUCATIONAL PARKS

The *extended neighborhood* notion was proposed to the federal district court of Judge Carl Rubin as a method for desegregating the public schools of Dayton, Ohio. Since 1976 it has also been proposed in other places. Basically, the idea is to expand the definition of an appropriate attendance area in which a child may attend school. The extended neighborhood is defined so that it encompasses a population that satisfies the racial ratio desired for the school system and also is composed of contiguous housing areas. Once the boundaries of this new attendance area have been established, the school population might extend to as many as 8000 students.

Ideally, each school within the extended neighborhood would have a unique magnet program organized. Parents of students would be given the option to select the educational program they wanted their child to have. The child would then be assigned to that program, but he or she would remain within the extended neighborhood. In a sense, parents would make a forced choice about the educational experiences they would like their child to have. School authorities would assign children to programs of the parents' choice, but with the controlling factor of racial balance. An example of how an extended neighborhood operates follows:

> The defined extended neighborhood encompasses 5000 elementary students and 6 elementary school buildings. The racial composition of the school system is 60 percent white and 40 percent black. The racial composition of the extended neighborhood as defined is 58 percent white and 42 percent black. The six schools of the extended neighborhood are designated as follows:
>
> School A: Traditional program
> School B: IGE program
> School C: Fine arts program
> School D: Career opportunities program
> School E: Math–science program
> School F: Open-spaced school program
>
> Parents are allowed to select one of the six school programs provided. Once the parents select a program, the students are assigned to a school, with one of the controlling factors being racial balance of the school.

It can be seen from the above example that the elements of both choice and arbitrary assignment exist in the extended neighborhood concept. The extended neighborhood allows students to remain in a neighborhood, albeit an expanded one. It allows parents an element of choice in the education they want their child to have, and it allows a school system to effectively desegregate its population programmatically rather than by the arbitrary assignment of youngsters strictly on a racial basis. This concept requires much careful planning and is administratively more complicated than the simple residential assignment of students to schools.

One example of an extensively expanded neighborhood is the *educational park*, a concept that has had limited implementation but offers great promise as a viable desegregated educational alternative. The park is the final phase of the extended neighborhood and includes a group of buildings designed to serve 7000 to 10,000 students on a single site. In each building are offered a variety of educational programs. Once the student arrives at the park site, he or she is assigned to a specific school building and participates in the educational programs offered in that building.

The educational park with its collection of individual school buildings provides centrally housed physical education, music, media, and dining facilities. These centralized facilities, in and of themselves, represent enormous savings because they eliminate the duplication that would exist with a series of small schools located throughout the city. The educational park has the added advantage of a single centralized administrative staff and a centralized maintenance and support staff.

Additionally, the educational park allows a community to provide first-rate facilities, especially in high-cost educational programs. The apparatus and facilities needed for programs in physical education, industrial arts, and home management, for example, fall in the high-cost area but are essential for a complete and well-rounded educational program. Additionally, the need to duplicate materials in a media center is greatly reduced, and though the single facility must be expanded to accommodate 10,000 students or more, it still requires less duplication than ten single facilities servicing smaller populations. The educational park also offers an opportunity to consolidate administrative offices and thus employ fewer personnel and more highly trained administrative and support personnel.

The educational park also affords an opportunity to locate on a single site various social and community services that directly relate to the students of the community. Currently, it is common to delay or even forego needed psychological, psychiatric, and family services in individual schools because of their scattered locations within the community.

A final advantage to the educational park is that the starting time for instruction can be scheduled so that it does not conflict with the general "starting time" of the community. Most places are "eight o'clock towns" or "nine o'clock towns." School hours can be scheduled so as not to conflict with the usual business opening and closing times, and the existing community transportation system can be used during nonpeak times. This would allow the community to realize maximum utilization of public transportation and avoid the cost of duplicating transportation, personnel, and equipment.

The educational park is, in a sense, a school facility modeled after a college or university. A series of buildings each provide educational programs for a clearly identified group of youngsters. The advantage of the park is that there is a centralization of facilities and programs with the opportunity to offer wide choices in the programs and the opportunity to achieve economies in the expensive components of educational program. The park allows for all children within a defined, although expanded, geographic area to attend school on the same site. This permits school officials to adjust building populations in order to maintain a racial balance that reflects the overall racial balance of the extended neighborhood.

The initial cost of an educational park is high. It was determined in 1976 that a park for 10,000 students constructed in a southwestern Ohio city would cost roughly $28 million. Inflation requires us to say that the cost has risen, but it is still within range of most communities. Once the initial cost is paid, important savings occur in actual operation by consolidating maintenance and supplies. Cost saving is also realized because of the centralization of staff and the reduction of administrative and supervisory personnel.

The educational park is a new concept. It may seem radical, but in this era of large consolidated industries, housing tracts, apartment complexes, and mass transportation, the notion of bigness is more commonplace than the notion of smallness. The "bigness" of a properly organized educational park can provide high-quality educational programs, allow the school to address more precisely the individual needs of various students, and provide the flexibility in school programming that is now missing in the "neighborhood school." Large units can be organized so that an important sense of intimacy is maintained. The "school within a school" concept is one such answer.[12]

METROPOLITANISM

The desegregation planner must always be aware of the latest efforts by other planners and the latest court decision about particular directions or strategies. To go far beyond the boundary of the latest directions given by planners or courts will cause the planner to represent the client in a less than optimal manner. A desegregation plan on the cutting edge of social innovation could be thrown out because the court has not spoken to the issue.

Metropolitan remedies for desegregation present such a case. Several experts in the field of desegregation have called for metropolitan remedies and have gone so far as to say that the metropolitan approach is the only way to resolve the segregated problem of large cities.[13] Nevertheless, we must be aware of what the courts are saying and also understand exactly what the issue is.

Primarily, the metropolitan concept arose out of popular social and political thought in the late 1960s and early '70s. There was growing concern among city planners and public school officials and ethnic action groups that the cities were growing more black by the day and soon would be made up predominantly of one race. They also observed cities that were in the process of desegregating, an activity that seemed to speed the departure of whites from the city. They observed that most of the suburbs surrounding the city were predominantly white. For example, Richmond, Virginia, in the late 1960s was 80 percent black, whereas surrounding Chesterfield, Henrico, and Hanover counties were either all white or predominantly white. They also could see that city and suburbs were connected in ways that truly represented metropolitan thinking (i.e., business, industry, sharing of services, and a highway system that established the city as the hub of the metropolitan area). It seemed to these planners that the only way to have the city remain vital as a metropolitan center was to move beyond the boundaries of the immediate political subdivision and include the surrounding suburbs. The desire to accomplish this was greater than a desire for school desegregation. It extended to concern for the revitalization of the city.[14]

The Supreme Court spoke directly to the school desegregation aspect of the issue in one large city. In Detroit, the eighty-six suburban districts had been joined in *Bradley* v. *Milliken* when District Judge Roth declared that "relief of segregation in the public schools of the City of Detroit cannot be accomplished within the corporate geographical limits of the city." Ultimately, fifty-six suburban districts were included in the order, and these districts appealed the decision. On appeal, the Supreme Court established that

... before the boundaries of separate and autonomous school districts may be set aside by consolidating the separate units for remedial purposes or by imposing an inter-district remedy, it must first be shown that there has been a constitutional violation within one district that produces a significant segregating effect in another district.

In other words, the Court said that unless it could be established that the actions of one district directly contributed to the segregation of another district, the Court could not make them a part of the remedy.[15]

The direction given in *Milliken* has been the principle on which courts have responded to other proposals for metropolitan desegregation. Wilmington, Delaware, courts found that the county surrounding Wilmington did in fact contribute to the segregation of Wilmington's public schools. But, the courts did not accept a metropolitan plan; they only requested that one be proposed.[16] In *U.S.* v. *Missouri*,[17] a remedy involving three separate districts was ordered after an examination of the evidence. The court found, applying the principle of *Milliken*, that the state had behaved in such a way that it had caused the area to be racially segregated. The court consolidated all districts involved and established a uniform tax rate.

Some may look on the Jefferson County–Louisville, Kentucky, case[18] as a metropolitan issue, but this was a merger effected under Kentucky law. Through merger, Jefferson County and Louisville were consolidated into one political subdivision for purposes of education, and the new district was desegregated by court order. It would be interesting to see if the two districts had been joined in a metropolitan plan whether or not the court would have had to apply the principles of *Milliken.*

The only instance where a true interdistrict remedy has been prescribed is in Indianapolis.[19] This case began in the 1960s with litigation against the Board of School Commissioners. It included charges of segregation of faculty and students, which were dealt with separately. The case involving the students is *U.S.* v. *Board of School Commissioners of the City of Indianapolis, Indiana.*

Through a series of legislative acts from those which, up until 1949, required segregation to the 1969 Uni-Gov act, which permitted metropolitan civil government but inhibited metropolitan school district development, a history of segregative acts both pre- and post-*Brown* were shown to have occurred. The Indianapolis "school-city" thus was mostly black, while the unified Indianapolis city, which was composed of the central city plus surrounding Marion County, reflected not a mixed population but a series of independent white suburban school districts.

The district court first found that a desegregation remedy would have to include all of Marion County. *Milliken* was applied on appeal, and the case was remanded to the district court. On this remand the district court found two constitutional violations that it felt warranted an interdistrict remedy: (1) there was the failure of the Indiana legislature to extend the boundaries of the "school city" when the governmental units of the county were consolidated; and (2) there was the failure of the housing authority to locate public housing beyond the former boundaries of Indianapolis.

An interdistrict remedy was ordered. It provided for busing that would result in each suburban district having a 15 percent black student body. Future construction of public housing within the former boundaries of Indianapolis was prohibited. This decision was sustained by the Seventh Circuit Court of Appeals.

The U.S. Supreme Court later vacated the decision and remanded the case for further consideration in the light of two other cases.[20] But this was not the end. In April 1979 the district court, on consideration of the particulars, determined that segregative intent had been shown. Eight suburban districts were required to participate in the desegregation of Indianapolis by means of a one-way busing plan. The specifics of that plan are being developed as this book is written.

A case currently in litigation in which a metropolitan remedy is being proposed is in Benton Harbor, Michigan.[21] In the trial court the judge declared two rural districts liable for having contributed to the segregation of Benton Harbor. On order for remedy, he asked a court-appointed committee to look at the best way to correct this violation. A metropolitan plan has been submitted to the court by one of the parties. The liability issue is on appeal to the Sixth Circuit, and remedies have yet to be submitted and studied by the court. One of the more interesting parts of this case is that Benton Harbor is a small city, and the other districts in Berrien County are mostly rural farming areas. They are not connected for business, industrial, or other reasons, thereby eliminating them from consideration as a metropolitan area. The issue here is whether the violation is sufficient[22] to cause the court to issue a cross- or interdistrict remedy, not a metropolitan remedy. The court is basing its position on a 1976 decision by the Supreme Court relating to metropolitan desegregation of Chicago public housing. In this case, *Hills v. Gautreaux,*[23] the Court found that the Chicago Housing Authority, which has jurisdiction over metropolitan Chicago, was deliberately selecting sites for public housing in a black ghetto, thereby avoiding integrated housing. The Court applied *Milliken* and ordered HUD and the CHA to provide metropolitan relief for this constitutional violation.

As one can see, the above information would and should seriously condition a planner's thought process. It seems that both *Brinkman* (how far?) and *Milliken* (show the contribution) are the principles to follow. One should also consider the feasibility of linking school districts that have no common fabric for linkage. Is the area a metropolitan area, or is it merely a group of districts that are contiguous?

Metropolitan planning for desegregation is still in its early stages, and it will proceed slowly. The most effective political governmental units to cause this to take effect on a broad scale are legislatures and state boards of education. Local districts were established as political subdivisions for education to carry out a state constitutional mandate, free public education. It is within the power of these units to reestablish these subdivisions. Until that time, planners will and should be reluctant to draw plans that extend beyond a school district's boundary.

This chapter has attempted to bring certain issues into clearer focus. The chapter opened with an examination of *integration,* distinguishing it from the sheer body mixing that is *desegregation.* The difficulty in achieving an integrated setting is great, although such an effort can begin to occur only after schools have been desegregated.

Segregation may occur not only along racial and ethnic lines; certain school practices also often result in economic and intellectual segregation. Although the decisions are somewhat less obvious, courts have been known to speak to these issues. Desegregation planners would be well advised to adjust proposals to reduce the possibility of extensive segregation of various economic levels by examining certain community demographics. To educators in the school district falls the task of ensuring educational equity and reducing the negative impact of intellectual segregation. This does not suggest that programs for the talented and the less able should not continue when appropriate (although this decision may become one that educators may have to share with the legislative and judicial sectors). It does suggest that children learn much from one another, cognitively and affectively, and a program characterized by rigid tracking is suspect educationally and judicially.

Efforts to desegregate, much less to integrate, are confounded by current population shifts ranging from marked population decline in some school districts to continued movement to suburban locales (often called "white flight" but frequently better labeled as "class flight") to a dramatic influx of people to the sunbelts. There is evidence that some cities may enter a renaissance; an in-migration seems to be occurring here and there, perhaps encouraged more by energy shortages than by far-sighted renewal programs. Nevertheless, shifting populations result in school closings, and there does seem to be a surge of movement by some segments of the population in the first years of desegregation.

Numerous solutions to the problem of school desegregation have been tried with varying degrees of success and varying degrees of acceptance by courts, the public, and educators. Some solutions although appealing and seemingly theoretically sound, have not been efficacious. Volunteerism, for example, has a pleasant ring, and innovative programs in magnet schools would seem to make educational sense, but neither has been an effective desegregative tool. The fact is, given the historically segregated nature of housing, there seems to be no way short of massive pupil transportation to effect massive desegregation. Organizational schemes such as educational parks, extended neighborhoods, and the participation of the suburbs in the desegregation of cities offer promise, but these solutions cannot be effective without enlarging the numbers of pupils transported.

The remainder of this book discusses in greater detail, each of the issues presented in this chapter, attempting to place in perspective the choices available and the consequences of various actions. There is no simple solution, just as there is no perfect solution. The challenge to the desegregation planner is to focus on the maximum feasible solution within the law. It is not a challenge that is easily met.

SELECTED COURT DECISIONS

Alexander v. *Holmes County Board of Education,* 396 U.S. 19 (1969).

U.S. v. *Board of School Commissioners of the City of Indianapolis,* 410 U.S. 909 (1973); 502 F.2d 68 (1974); 541 F.2d 1211 (1976); 97 S.Ct. 802 (1977).

Dayton Board of Education v. *Brinkman,* 518 F.2d 853 (6th Cir., 1975); Cert. Denied 423 U.S. 1000 (1975); 97 S.Ct. 2766 (1977).

Milliken v. *Bradley,* 418 U.S. 717 (1974).

Hills v. *Gautreaux,* 94 S.Ct. 1538 (1976).

Swann v. *Charlotte-Mecklenburg,* 402 U.S. 1 (1971).

Arlington Heights v. *Metropolitan Housing Development Corporation,* 97 S.Ct. 555 (1977).

Keyes v. *School District No. 1,* 413 U.S. 189 (1973).

Pasadena City Board of Education v. *Spangler,* 427 U.S. 424 (1976).

BIBLIOGRAPHY

A Citizen's Guide to School Desegregation Law. Washington, D.C.: National Institute of Education, July 1978.

Clark, Kenneth. *Dark Ghetto.* New York: Harper & Row, 1965.

Forehand, Garlie A., et al., *Conditions and Processes of Effective School Desegregation. Final Report for USOE.* Princeton, N.J.: Educational Testing Service, 1976. (ED 131 154)

Gordon, Edmund. *A Comparative Study of Quality Integrated Education. Final Report for NIE.* New York: Institute for Urban and Minority Education, Columbia University, 1976. (ED 128 546)

Hodges, Harold. *Underdogs, Middle Americans, and Elites: Structural Inequality in the United States.* Morristown, N.J.: General Learning Press, 1976.

Hughes, Larry W. *Informal and Formal Community Forces: External Influences on Schools and Teachers.* Morristown, N.J.: General Learning Press, 1976.

Hughes, Larry W. and Gerald C. Ubben, *The Elementary School Principal's Handbook: Guide to Effective Action,* Boston: Allyn and Bacon, 1978.

Nevas, Susan R. "Factors in Desegregation and Integration." Eric Clearinghouse for Urban Education. New York: Columbia University, Fall 1977.

Orstein, Allan. "Busing: The Issue That Will Not Go Away." *Carnegie Quarterly* 36, no. 2 (Spring 1978).

Pettigrew, Thomas. *A Study of School Integration. Final Report for U.S. DHEW.* Cambridge, Mass.: Harvard University Press, 1970. (ED–044–468)

Sanders, Stanley and Janice Yarborough. "Achieving a Learning Environment with ORDER." *Clearing House* 50, no. 3 (November 1976): 100–102.

Weinberg, Morris. "Desegregation Research: An Appraisal." *Phi Delta Kappan* 59, no. 3. (November 1977).

NOTES

1. *Brown* v. *Board of Education of Topeka,* 347 U.S. 483 (1954).

2. Susan Nevas, "Factors in Desegregation and Integration," *Equal Opportunity Review,* Eric Clearinghouse for Urban Education, Columbia University, Fall 1977.

3. Kenneth B. Clark, *Dark Ghetto* (New York: Harper & Row, 1965), pp. 232–233.

4. Ibid., p. 234.

5. Morris Weinberg, "Desegregation Research: An Appraisal," *Phi Delta Kappan,* 59, no. 3 (November 1977).

6. Thomas Pettigrew, *A Study of School Integration. Final Report for the U.S. Department of Health, Education, and Welfare under Contract No. OEC–1–6–61774–1887,. Cooperative Research Project No. 6–1774* (Cambridge, Mass.: Harvard University, 1970). (ED 044 468)

7. Edmund Gordon, *A Comparative Study of Quality Integrated Education. Final Report for NIE under Grant No. NE–G–00–3–156. Project 3–1495* (New

York: Institute for Urban and Minority Education, Teachers College, Columbia University, 1976). (ED 128 546)

8. Garlie A. Forehand, et al., *Conditions and Processes of Effective School Desegregation. Final Report for U.S. Office of Education Contract OEC–O–73–6341* (Princeton, N.J.: Educational Testing Service, 1976). (ED 131 154)

9. Some cities, Houston is one, offset this with vigorous annexation. There is some indication, too, that suburban spread may be retarded by the energy shortage.

10. See Larry W. Hughes and Gerald C. Ubben, *The Elementary Principal's Handbook: Guide to Effective Action,* (Boston: Allyn and Bacon, 1978). Chapter 31 details specific ways to make good use of citizen groups.

11. An excellent example is the Chicago schools' "Accent on Excellence." This program is designed to allow students to select special schools that have special educational programs. Though several thousand students have chosen to become involved in these programs, they make up a small percentage of the nearly 500,000 students in the Chicago school system. Chicago is not unique in its experience. Most schools with voluntary programs have levels of participation that approximate the Chicago experience.

12. Stanley Sanders and Janice Yarborough, "Achieving a Learning Environment with ORDER," *Clearing House* 50, no. 3 (November 1976): 100–102.

13. Allan Orfield, "Busing: The Issue That Will Not Go Away," *Carnegie Quarterly* 36 no. 2 (Spring 1978).

14. Many black leaders also were concerned that the all-black city had given extensive political power to blacks and that the inclusion of whites would dilute that power.

15. *Milliken* v. *Bradley,* 418 U.S., at 744–45.

16. *Evans* v. *Buchanan,* 423 U.S. 963 (1976). What eventually developed was not an interdistrict plan, however. A new school district was formed, entitled New Castle County Schools, which embraced the metropolitan area.

17. 515 F.2d 1365 (8 Cir., 1975).

18. *Newburg Area Council* v. *Board of Education,* 418 U.S. 919 (1974).

19. *U.S.* v. *Board of School Commissioners of the City of Indianapolis,* 410 U.S. 909 (1973); 502 F.2d 68 (1974); F.2d 1211 (1976); 97 S.Ct. 802 (1977).

20. *Village of Arlington Heights* v. *Metropolitan Housing Authority,* 429 U.S. (1977); and *Washington* v. *Davis,* 429 U.S. 229 (1976). Both cases hold that a showing of disparate impact alone is not enough to show segregative intent. Segregative intent must also be alleged and proved.

21. *Berry* v. *School District of the City of Benton Harbor,* (W. D. Michigan, in process).

22. See *Dayton Board of Education* v. *Brinkman,* 97 S.Ct. 2766 (1977).

23. *Hills* v. *Gautreaux,* 94 S.Ct. 1538, (1976).

3

Reading and Interpreting
a Court Order

It is important for the desegregation planner to understand the mandates of
the courts when a school system has been found guilty of racially segregating
its schools. All too often, school systems find themselves in difficulty because
they attempt to read and interpret a court order as narrowly as possible. It is
not uncommon to hear school officials or their attorneys put great emphasis
on a single word or phrase in their efforts to interpret the court order in
terms of their own personal feelings. This is generally a mistake because it
puts the school board in an adversary position with the courts, and in many
cases it puts the school system in a position of violating the spirit of the
court order. There is ample evidence of school systems that have so antago-
nized the court with their narrow interpretations that extreme remedies have
been directed in place of more logical approaches built on reasonable com-
promises.

For purposes of illustration this chapter uses the decision by Judge Robert Duncan of the U.S. District Court for the Southwest District of Ohio,
Eastern Division. The civil action that this decision is based on is *Gary L.
Penick et al.* v. *The Columbus Board of Education, et al.*[1] The basic outline of
the court order is followed by excerpts used to illustrate points.

OPINION AND ORDER

This brief section identifies the judge and states the matter before the courts.
Generally, this is a concise statement made in standard language. In this
case the statement is

> *Duncan, District Judge.* This matter is before the Court following trial on the issue
> of liability. The Court sets forth hereinbelow its findings of facts and conclusions
> of law, in accordance with 52(*a*) of the Federal Rules of Civil Procedure.

This brief statement states that the federal judge having jurisdiction over the case is District Judge Robert Duncan. The court has under its jurisdiction a civil matter, and this document has been issued following the trial and speaks to the issue of liability.

The court establishes that the document contains two major elements: (1) the "findings of fact," which is the evidence presented to the court that pertains directly to the court's decision and (2) the "conclusions of law," which is the decision that the court has made in terms of the evidence presented and bounded by existing federal statutes for constitutional law.

INTRODUCTION

Opening Statement

The introduction of the court order establishes if there is culpability on the part of the defendants. Judge Duncan states that. . . "after having considered evidence and applied what I understand to be the law of the United States, I conclude that the *plaintiffs are entitled* to judgement" (italics added).

Thus the court states immediately that the plaintiff, *Gary L. Penick et al.* (i.e., the group of plaintiffs, one of whom is Gary L. Penick), who has brought this action against the Columbus Board of Education, is entitled to remedy. Following this statement, and in the same paragraph, the court further states that . . . "it is the duty of the court to set forth the *reasons* for arriving at that conclusion." (italics added).

Judge Duncan has now established that the group represented by Penick is entitled to judgment against the Columbus Board of Education and that the court is now going to present the reaons why Penick is entitled to a judgment.

The court then establishes that this order is written in a language that individuals other than attorneys will be able to read and understand. The court also is cognizant of the fact that this is a legal opinion and, therefore, must stand the scrutiny of the legal profession. Thus, Judge Duncan states:

> . . . on the other hand, the court cannot evade its responsibility to counsel in this case who have worked long, hard and sincerely in behalf of their clients. The legal authorities in precedence under which the court relies must be communicated to the lawyers. To facilitate a reading and understanding of this opinion, the court has prepared an appendix containing a glossary of terms and a few maps.

The court has now established that, like a textbook, the document can be read and understood by a layman but that provisions have been made for a more sophisticated reading through the use of appendixes.

In the remainder of the opening statement Judge Duncan establishes the right of the federal court to adjudicate this case and gives some philosophical overtones of desegregation in general. The court uses as its reference point *Brown* v. *Board of Education,* 347 U.S. 483 (1954). This is a fairly standard reference point and is found in many federal desegregation cases.

Procedural History

Once a court has made its introductory statements, it is prepared to examine the history to date of this particular piece of litigation. Additionally, the court establishes the laws and identifies the parties to the case.

> . . . the court has jurisdiction of the issues pursuant to 28 U.S. C. 1331(*a*) and 1343 (3) and (4). The Civil Rights claimed to have been violated are those secured by the *Equal Protection Clause of the 14th Amendment* of the United States Constitution. (Italics added)

This reference to the Fourteenth Amendment is a basic reference and underlies school desegregation cases adjudicated at the federal level. Following this jurisdictional statement, the court establishes who the parties at trial in this case are.

1. *Intervening plaintiffs.* These are plaintiffs who have joined the litigation after the initial filing. In this case the intervening plaintiffs are eleven students who attend schools in the Columbus public school system. They represent a class of persons and were permitted to join the litigation in March 1975.

2. *Original plaintiffs.* This is a group of fourteen students and their parents who originally filed against the Columbus Public Schools. This group of plaintiffs also represented a class of people who felt their right of equal access to public education was being denied them by the Columbus public schools. The original plaintiffs are also identified as presenting evidence not included within the case presented by the intervening plaintiffs.

3. *Columbus defendants.* This group is made up of the Columbus Board of Education, its seven elected members, and Dr. John Ellis, Superintendent of Columbus public schools.

4. *State defendants.* This group is identified as the State Board of Education, State Superintendent of Public Instruction, Governor of the State of Ohio, and Attorney General of the State of Ohio.

The plaintiffs thus become two groups: the intervening plaintiffs, consisting of eleven students; and the original plaintiffs, consisting of fourteen students. These two groups both claim discriminatory acts on the part of the defendants. They present evidence that differs on certain issues, and thus they become two distinct groups. This also allows the newer group, the intervening plaintiffs, to keep the case from becoming moot through the matriculation of students in the original plaintiff group.

The defendants are defined as the Columbus school officials, the state's school officials, and the governor and the attorney general of Ohio. Again, in order to maintain litigation, the defendants are identified individually by name and individually by position. Thus, if one of the plaintiffs should leave office, the litigation against that office would still be intact.

The court further establishes that the case was filed on June 21, 1973, by Gary L. Penick and thirteen other children who were students in the Columbus school system. It establishes that on October 9, 1973, a preliminary injunction to stop a construction program was filed and heard by Judge Carl B. Rubin on April 15 and 17, 1974. Following this were some amended complaints that first dismissed the state defendants and then renamed the state defendants, plus adding as a defendant the Franklin County recorder.

Allegations of the complainants were

> ... that the Columbus defendants had intentionally segregated the public schools by creating and maintaining a neighborhood school policy notwithstanding a segregated housing pattern of the city. The new school construction program was claimed to further segregation ... by using optional attendance areas, by segregating teachers and principals, by failing to desegregate and by conspiring with the County Recorder to violate the fair housing law of 1968. ...

This section concludes by stating that

> ... the trial commenced on April 19, 1976 and was completed on June 17, 1976 ... over 70 witnesses were heard and over 600 exhibits were admitted. The trial transcription is in excess of 6600 pages ... court heard closing arguments ... on September 3, 1976.

This summary statement simply establishes the kind of record developed in the course of this litigation.

PRE–1954 HISTORY

The court now establishes the history of the segregation of the Columbus public schools prior to 1954. Again the reason for the selection of 1954 is because of the precedent case of *Brown* v. *Board of Education.* This section is a picture and is used to "visit with the history of the system ... neither for the purpose of dragging out skeletons of the past nor a vindictive finger pointing exercise."

The court then looks back to 1871. It cites some early litigation and an Ohio law that authorized local boards of education to organize separate schools for "colored" children (House Bill 105, 75 Ohio L. 513, 1878). This law, as pointed out by the court, was repealed in 1887 (84, Ohio L. 34) and was sustained by the Ohio Supreme Court in 1888 in the case of *Board of Education* v. *The State,* 45 Ohio St. 555.

The history goes on to describe when the first black person graduated from high school in Columbus, when separate schools for black children were abolished in Columbus, when schools were built in predominantly black residential districts and staffed with black teachers, when school attendance areas were gerrymandered so that the races could remain separate, and instances in which 100 percent white faculties were transferred and replaced by 100 percent black faculties. The court concludes this section by stating:

> ... in 1954 the Columbus defendants' predecessors had caused some black children to be educated in schools that were predominantly white; however, the Board *deliberately caused* at least 5 schools to be overwhelmingly black while

drawing some attendance zones to allow white students to avoid these black schools.
(Italics added)

The court has now established that the Columbus defendants deliberately caused the schools to be segregated through the assignment of students and through the drawing of attendance zones. Again, it must be kept in mind that the court has established that these acts happened prior to 1954 and thus prior to the first *Brown* decision.

POST–1954 HISTORY

An Overview

The court then proceeds to look at the history of the Columbus public schools since 1954, the year of the first *Brown* decision. The court begins this section by describing the growth of the Columbus community and emphasizes the sharp increase in population, both black and white. The court also establishes that the increase in black population was disproportionate to that of white population, the black population growing from 11.7 percent in 1940 to 18.5 percent in 1970. The court concedes that significant residential variation occurred during that period with 71 percent of all the blacks living in Columbus residing within twenty-three contiguous census tracts.

The history of the system relates that by 1956 there were still no black administrators in any but all-black schools and no white principals in black schools and that "between 1964 and 1973 the Columbus defendants generally maintained their prior practice of assigning black teachers to those schools with substantial black student populations."

The history of the system then progresses through the establishment of the Council of Intercultural Education, agreements between the Columbus defendants, and the Ohio Civil Rights Commission, the history of the series of defeated school bond issues, and finally the development of the "Columbus Plan." The Columbus Plan is an attempt to resolve some of the racial imbalances through a variety of student transfers on a voluntary basis. The court concludes:

> ... nevertheless during the 1975–76 school year, when this case was tried, 70.4% of all the students in the Columbus Public Schools attended schools which were 80 to 100% populated by either black or white students; 73.3% of the black administrators were assigned to schools with 70–100% black student bodies; and 95.7% of the 92 schools which were 80–100% white had no black administrators assigned to them.

The court in this summary statement establishes that the school system is still in a segregated posture and that assignments of students and administrators seem to be influenced by the race of the individuals involved.

Specific Actions

At the beginning of this section, the court reminds itself that "the court has not forgotten the truism that the mere presence of racial imbalance and the makeup of school student bodies, without more, will not permit a finding of unconstitutional segregation." With this acknowledgement the court proceeds to establish those specific acts committed by the defendants that have caused racial identifiability and have thus obviated the right of equal access to the education institutions of Columbus, Ohio.

The court first cites the site selection for school buildings and concludes that the evidence shows that in many cases alternative site selections were suggested that would have precluded racially identifiable schools.

> ... the evidence supports the finding that the Columbus defendants could have reasonably foreseen the probable racial composition of schools to be constructed on given site. In some instances the Columbus defendants had actual knowledge of the likelihood that some schools would open and remain racially identifiable if built on the proposed site.

The court goes on to cite specific schools that were built where the racial identifiability of the population was known. Judge Duncan cites several instances and then elaborates on his reasons why the racial identifiability of each would be known.

The court acknowledges the Columbus defendants' position that the housing patterns of the city were segregative and that in order to maintain the neighborhood school policy, certain schools by default would be single-raced. The court answers this contention by stating that "the evidence shows that in some instances the need for school facilities could have been met in a manner having an integrative rather than segregative effect."

After the court establishes that the school authorities had flexibility in building construction that would have had a desegregative effect on the school community, it proceeds to the citing of several specific acts of segregation on the part of the school authorities. For each act the court presents a brief history, examines the consequences, and then responds to the arguments of both defendants and plaintiffs. Throughout the summarization of these acts the court references both intent and outcomes in terms of racial balances, staff assignments, and effects on the racial isolation within the community. The court references five such identifiable acts.

CONSTITUTIONAL QUESTIONS
The Concept of Intent

The court begins this section by setting forth a number of general legal propositions it will use as guidelines. The court states that "in order to receive any remedial action from the courts, plaintiffs must show their constitutional rights have been violated." The court then cites *Keyes* v. *School District No. 1*, 413 U.S. 189, 198 (1973).

Once Judge Duncan establishes his baseline with *Keyes,* he proceeds to develop a legal basis for the establishment of intent. At this point in the opinion the court relies heavily on footnotes with excerpts from decisions that pertain to school segregation. These citations are legalistic and are designed to provide the legal scholar or attorney with points of reference that will allow research of this and subsequent litigation.

Inference of Segregative Intent

Here again the court summarizes the defendants' argument that much of the segregation is caused by housing patterns and the fact that the school board was operating under a neighborhood school philosophy. The plaintiffs counter that much of the segregation has arisen out of a series of board actions both remote and recent.

The court responds to the above positions by stating that ". . . various segments of the community, notably black parents and civic organizations, repeatedly and articulately vocalized concern, anguish or dismay concerning both overtly desegregative action and lost integrative opportunities."

The court, once it has established the position that the school board in fact was aware that some of its acts were causing segregation in the community, goes on to recant some of the testimony provided throughout the trial.

The court then addresses the neighborhood school concept and residential segregation. Through these citations the court refers to prior federal and state decisions, and while acknowledging these as probable concerns or mitigating circumstances, it acknowledges that alternatives were available that could have been pursued logically.

Judge Duncan then looks at the recent efforts on the part of the Columbus defendants. He cites several innovative educational alternatives—the balancing of the teaching staff and attempts to recruit additional black faculty and administrators. He commends the defendants for these positive efforts, but then, by again citing *Keyes,* he establishes that the defendants' evidence fell short of showing that the racial character of the school system is not the result of racially neutral social dynamics. Thus, he finds the defendants guilty of segregative racial intent.

The State Defendants

The court also finds the state's defendants culpable because "at no time have these state defendants actively moved to do anything to correct the racial imbalance in the Columbus schools." The court goes on to state:

> . . . the court is of the opinion that the law of Ohio requires the State Board of Education to assure that school children in the various local school districts enjoy a full range of constitutional rights. The Board has not done this in Columbus even though it has received sufficient statistical evidence of student and faculty

racial imbalance and is well aware of existence of racially imbalanced schools in Columbus.

The court concludes that "the State Board and State Superintendent are Ohio's resident experts on school desegregation matters."

CONCLUSION

In this section the court concludes the burden of guilt. The court cites other litigation that serves as precedent and establishes rules of law that the court is now following. There is a brief summary and the establishment of some philosophical positions pertaining to the court's view of school segregation and the concepts of equal access to education.

ORDER

This is the point where the court directs the defendants, who have been ad-juged culpable, to provide a remedy to the segregation that currently exists in the school system. The court begins its order by saying:

The court finds the issue joined in favor of all named plaintiffs and the class or classes they represent, and against defendants . . . Board of Education and its members, Superintendent of . . . Public Schools, the State Board of Education . . . and the State Superintendent of Public Instruction.

The court then proceeds to render a judgment against the defendants. Specifically, in the Columbus, Ohio, case the court found:

1. The Clerk will award all plaintiffs and the class or classes they represent those costs which are allowable to prevailing plaintiffs under the acceptable law.

2. The cost will be borne equally by the Board of Education, and the State Board of Education.

3. The defendants Columbus Board of Education, State Board of Education, their Constituent members, officers, agents, servants, employees, and all other persons in active concert or participation with them be and they are hereby *permanently enjoined from discriminating on the basis of race in the operation of Columbus Public Schools.* (Italics added)

4. Defendants Columbus Board of Education and State Board of Education are *directed to formulate and submit* to the court proposed *plans for the desegrega-tion of the Columbus Public Schools* beginning with the 1977–78 school year. (Italics added)

5. [the plan must be submitted] within 90 days of the entry of this order . . .

6. . . . the Columbus Board of Education . . . is hereby *enjoined from proceeding with construction* of new schools or additions to existing schools unless such construction has already commenced. Hereafter such new construction may proceed only upon prior approval of this court. (Italics added)

The court has now established what it wants in terms of a remedy. The court has stated that the defendants are to submit plans for the desegregation of the schools and that those plans must be submitted within ninety days after the order. The court has also stated that the school board cannot enter into any new construction of buildings unless that construction is approved by the court. The court has now turned the problem of desegregation over to the defendants and has instructed them to proceed.

APPENDIX

The court frequently provides two appendixes to accompany the order. First, there is often a glossary. Most often, the significant factor in the glossary will be that the court will define racial identifiability in terms of the allowable percentages of white and black students within each building of the school system. The second appendix will frequently contain a series of maps that depict the various sections of the city and school attendance areas that have been addressed throughout the court order.

The reader can see that a court order establishing guilt will establish it at the onset. This will be followed by the reasoning the court has used and will look at the history of the case as it has been developed through the evidence. Following the history of the case, the court looks to precedent law that would address similar legal issues and situations. Once the court has looked at the precedent law, it will draw its conclusions built on that law and on the evidence presented in the case. Finally, the court orders a remedy. The remedy is, in most instances, the portion of the court order that comes under the greatest legalistic scrutiny. In many cases the defendants will try to define this order narrowly and present to the court only those items addressed specifically by the court. This is entirely within the rights of the defendants, and in most cases is done under the direction of legal counsel. Care must be taken that the orders of the court are carried out and that the defendants do not put themselves in a position where they can be held in contempt of court because they have ignored or dealt inappropriately with the direction of the court.

SELECTED COURT DECISIONS

Bronson v. *Board of Education of the City School District of Cincinnati,* 525 F.2d 344 (1975); Cert. Denied, 425 U.S. 934 (1976).

Clemons v. *Board of Education of Hillsboro,* 228 F.2d 853, 859 (6th Cir. 1956).

Evans v. *Buchanan,* 393 F. Supp. 428, 447 (D. Del. 1975).

Higgins v. *Board of Education of City of Grand Rapids,* 508 F.2d 799, at 791, 792 (6th Cir. 1974).

United States v. *Board of School Commissions of the City of Indianapolis,* 332 F.Supp. 655, 681 (S.D. Ind. 1971).

SELECTED BIBLIOGRAPHY

Jones, R. S. "Racial Patterns and School District Policy." *Urban Education* 12 (October 1977): 297–312.

Orfield, Gary. "Desegregation and the Educational Process." *Law and Contemporary Problems* 39, no. 2 (1975).

Phillips, J. E. "Legal Requirement of Intent to Segregate: Some Observations." *NOLPE School Law Journal* 7, no. 2 (1977): 111–125.

NOTES

1. *Gary L. Penick et al.* v. *The Columbus Board of Education et al.*, 429 F.Supp. 229 (D.C. Ohio 1977). All quotations in this chapter are taken from this case.

4

Data Needed to Prepare
a Desegregation Plan

Before any desegregation plan can be written, certain basic data must be gathered so that realistic judgments can be made. The plan drawn will be governed directly by the direction of the court through its court order or by the direction of the school board through its statement of intent.

These data, though some facts may be in flux, must be fixed at a single time and treated as though they were unchanging. An example of this would be pupil population. The population in any school system varies from day to day, but for the purpose of plan development a single date must be selected and the student population at that date used as the official population for desegregation efforts. Of course, these data are updated at the time the plan is put into effect.

Primary emphasis should be on data accuracy. School data should be checked through several sources and cross-checked constantly as the planner proceeds to formulate the plan. When columns do not total accurately and figures do not cross-check, the plan, even though it might be a good one, is suspect and subject to criticism. It must be kept in mind, too, that any school desegregation plan causes change and thus is subject to controversy and criticism. Therefore, the data used must be unimpeachable and simply stated.

PUPIL POPULATION

An important set of data for any school desegregation plan is information about the pupil population. Most states have an official reporting date for school attendance. Generally, this date falls sometime during the first or second month of the school year. These official pupil-count reports are submitted to the state so that school systems can be reimbursed through the state's school-support plans. These reports normally require the pupil population to be identified by school, grade, and race. Because these are official reporting figures, they are the most desirable figures to use when formulating a desegregation plan.

In the event that the state does not require an "October or September Report," or if the official report required does not contain a pupil count by school, grade, and race, there is a report that each school system must supply annually to the Office of Civil Rights of the Department of Health, Education, and Welfare. This OCR report requires a pupil population count by building, grade, and race, but it further identifies pupil population in the five broad racial categories identified by the federal government (black, white, Asian, Native American, and Hispanic). This may be an unnecessarily fine breakdown for many desegregation plans. The planner should select the categories of black and nonblack or white and nonwhite if the desegregation is to accommodate a basically black/white mix. This is not to say that a desegregation plan should be drawn so that other minority groups lose their racial or ethnic identity or that these groups are ignored in the formulation of a plan. There are instances when these other racial groups figure prominently in the development of a desegregation plan, and their numbers must then be taken into full consideration.

Once the pupil population figures have been assembled, they become the official baseline student population figures for the desegregation plan. It should be stated in the plan that the student population figures reflect the school system on a specific date, though it is understood that these figures change on a daily basis. Once these official figures have been collected, they should be put in a form similar to table 4.1 and used exclusively throughout the plan.

SCHOOL PERSONNEL

Three categories of school personnel must be considered: certificated personnel, administrative personnel, and noncertificated personnel. Most court orders speak to one or all of these personnel categories, and so population data must be acquired for each group.

Certificated Personnel

Certificated personnel must be identified by race, grade, or subject, and building assignment. These data should also be as of a specific date. Official state reports are the best source for these data. If the state does not require an official reporting of certificated personnel, then a report from the central office of the school administration will suffice. Once these data are collected, they should be recorded in a form similar to table 4.2 and used as the official baseline data for the portion of the desegregation plan that deals directly with the certificated staff.

TABLE 4.1. Student Population for the Elementary Schools, October 1980

School	Capacity	EMR	Grades							Total	Black	Nonblack	% Black
			K/	1	2	3	4	5	6				
Adlai Stevenson	608	9	71	71	53	63	74	85	80	506	506	0	100
Alfred A. Benesch	715	13	116	127	109	79	92	68	69	715	715	0	100
Almira	828	—	129	109	99	89	94	93	95	708	5	703	.7
Andrew J. Rickoff	678	35	86	96	71	97	90	89	114	678	678	0	100
Anthony Wayne	670	6	190	118	119	72	93	83	70	670	651	19	97.2
William C. Bryant	452	29	72	49	51	52	40	53	64	410	0	410	0
William H. Brett	461	45	76	68	38	40	51	42	38	398	18	380	4.5
William H. McGuffey	369	—	51	62	50	39	92	—	—	320	195	125	60.9
William R. Harper	370	8	39	45	34	36	36	44	39	281	0	281	0
Willow	358	10	42	55	31	35	34	33	45	285	5	280	1.8
TOTALS		2,519	11,534	10,322	8,652	8,231	8,273	8,388	8,621	66,608	38,677	27,931	58.07

DATA SOURCE: *State Pupil Population Report*, October 1980. Capacity figures: *Local Board Building Report*, May 1977.

TABLE 4.2. Percentages of Minority and Nonminority Teachers Assigned to Elementary Schools

School	Teachers M^a	Teachers NM^a	Total Staff[b]	% M	% NM	Out of Balance[c]
Aaron Burr	16.47	7.60	19.07	60.14	39.85	X
A. G. Beal	9.00	27.40	36.40	24.72	75.27	X
Alfred	14.20	13.20	27.40	51.82	48.17	
A. J. Rickoff	18.10	9.66	27.76	65.20	34.79	X
Anthony Wayne	11.88	11.52	23.40	50.76	49.23	
Anton Vorak	17.60	7.70	25.30	69.56	30.43	X
Barkwell	4.34	12.34	16.68	26.01	73.98	X
Beekins	16.00	7.40	23.40	68.37	31.62	X
Boulevard	13.50	10.80	24.30	55.55	44.44	
Buckeye	11.24	11.84	23.08	48.70	51.30	
Charles	14.90	10.04	24.94	59.74	40.25	X
C. W. Chesnutt	7.80	11.00	18.80	41.48	58.51	
C. T. Brewer	5.40	7.66	13.06	41.34	58.65	
Clanton	19.60	11.80	31.40	62.42	37.58	X
Watson	8.32	10.30	18.62	44.68	55.31	
Washington Irving	16.00	6.00	22.00	72.72	27.27	
Washington Park	1.86	4.94	6.80	27.35	72.64	X
Willow	7.40	5.24	12.64	58.54	41.45	X
Woodland Hills	13.20	14.58	27.78	47.51	51.48	
Woolridge	5.26	2.76	8.02	65.58	34.41	X
TOTALS	532.15	463.20	995.35	53.46	46.53	

[a]M = minority; NM = nonminority.

[b]Fractions occur because some teachers are assigned to two or more buildings or have part-time administrative duties.

[c]A school is out of balance if it exceeds 48% minority or 52% majority with a 5% tolerance.

Administrative Personnel

The administrative personnel must be accounted for in the same manner as the teaching personnel. Administrators must be identified by race, sex, and building assignment. Additionally, central office administrators must be identified in the same manner. Quasi administrators like guidance counselors, special project directors, and librarians should also be accounted for in this category. Once these data are collected, a form similar to table 4.3 should be developed to reflect the composition of the administrative staff. These data, once recorded, become the official baseline data for that portion of the desegregation plan pertaining to the administrative staff.

Non-Certificated Staff

The concern for noncertificated staff is relatively new in the pursuit of court-ordered school desegregation. The reason for this interest is that many job classifications seem to be reserved for specific racial groups. Thus, students

TABLE 4.3. High School Building Administrative Teams by Minority/Nonminority and Position[a]

	Principal		Asst. Principal		Out of
School	M	NM	M	NM	Balance
Adams	1	0	2	3	
Booker T. Washington	1	0	2	1	
David T. Hughes	1	0	3	1	
Douglas	0	1	2	2	
Jackson	0	1	1	2	
Jane Addams	0	1	1	1	
Javits	0	1	4	1	
J. F. Kennedy	1	0	3	1	
John Hay	1	0	3	1	
Kevin	0	1	1	3	
Lincoln West	0	1	1	3	
M. L. King	0	1	1	1	
North Tech	.0	1	1	0	
South Tech	0	1	1	3	
Wayne	0	1	1	3	
TOTALS	5	10	27	26	

[a]Frequently personnel occupying highly visible positions such as guidance counselors will be included in this analysis and reported as a part of the administrative team. A third column is added and these are also included in the analysis except that even here one must insure appropriate attention to some degree of racial balance among both groups.

may associate only with white secretaries and black custodians. The courts are now taking into consideration these identifications and are asking that this personnel category become a part of desegregation plans.

Data about noncertificated staff should be recorded by job classification, building assignment, race, and sex. These data, once collected, should be put in a form similar to tables 4.4 and 4.5 and become the official baseline data for the desegregation plan.

PHYSICAL FACILITIES

A new phenomenon is becoming a factor in many urban school desegregation plans. Because of declining school enrollments, there are now underused school buildings. Thus, a part of many desegregation plans is the examination of existing facilities with the anticipation of taking the more obsolete or energy-inefficient facilities out of service. The planner must therefore collect the following data on each facility within the school system:

1. School enrollments by year for the preceding five years

2. The percent of enrollment change for each building over a five-year period

3. The design capacity for each building

4. The location and condition of existing temporary structures or classrooms

TABLE 4.4. Classified Personnel Employed in Elementary Schools by Race and Position

Schools	Clerical		Custodial		Cafeteria		Total	
	B	NB	B	NB	B	NB	B	NB
Alger	0	1	3	0	0	1	3	2
Hill	1	0	1	1	0	0	2	1
Arlington	0	2	3	0	0	1	3	3
Bander	0	1	3	0	0	1	3	
Barton	1	0	1	1	0	0		
Basely Park	1	0	2	1	1			1
Beaumont Acres	0	1	2	1		1	0	4
Arkinson	0	1				0	4	1
Brammel			4	1	0	1	4	4
			0	3	0	1	0	6
	0	1	3	0	0	1	3	2
Creek	0	1	2	1	0	0	2	2
Wilson	1	0	4	0	0	0	5	0
Winters	0	1	2	1	0	1	2	3
Wonderland	0	1	2	1	0	1	2	3
Young	0	3	6	5	0	1	6	8
Zinn	0	1	1	2	0	1	1	4
TOTAL	13	132	264	97	28	84	305	313
%	9.0	91.0	73.1	26.9	25.0	85.0	49.4	50.6

SOURCE: Division of Research.

5. The annual operating cost for each building

6. The annual energy cost for each building

7. The age of each building including the age of any additions or renovations of the building

8. The urban change that has occurred where the building is located

9. The conversion or recycling potential of each building

10. The desegregative impact that the closing of the building will have upon the student population

It should be noted that some of the above items are relatively subjective, whereas others simply require the collection of information. Table 4.6 depicts how these data can be recorded for use by the desegregation planner.

Note in table 4.6 that several ratios have been established. The necessity for these ratios occurs because of the differences in sizes of buildings and the necessity for having some standardized unit so that comparisons can be made. Thus, the cost of operation of each building is divided by the stated capacity of that building. This gives a "cost per unit of capacity" figure. In like manner, the cost of energy per building is divided by the stated capacity of that building, yielding the "energy cost per unit" of capacity. It is now possible to compare the various school buildings of the community with like measures.

TABLE 4.5. Composites Classified Personnel in School Buildings, by Race and Position

Schools	Clerical		Custodial		Cafeteria		Total		
	B	NB	B	NB	B	NB	B	NB	
Elementary	13	129	257	90	28	82	298	301	
Junior High	16	51	142	28	35	131	193	210	
High	11	78	130	57	26	95	167	230	
Special and Other	1	12	11	11	1	3	13	22	
TOTAL	41	270	540	186	90	311	671	763	1.434
%	13.2	86.8	74.4	25.6	22.4	77.6	46.8	53.2	

SOURCE: Division of Research.

Factors such as "urban change" refer to where a building is located, its accessibility, and its degree of obsolescence. These are subjective but nonetheless important judgments. A similar subjective judgment is the conversion or recycling potential of a building. There are times when the location of a facility is such that its sale could yield a substantial sum to the school system and at the same time remove from service an obsolete facility. Another recycling potential is the conversion of urban facilities into adult education centers or centers for community or social services. A more detailed discussion of building closings can be found in chapter 6.

TRANSPORTATION

Transportation is one of the last components of a desegregation plan. The pupil-assignment process must be complete and the total number of children to be transported established before the actual transportation plan can be formulated.

A desegregation plan is composed of several parts. These parts are interdependent, but because of its nature, the transportation plan must occur after student assignments are made. While the planner is making judgments pertaining to student assignment, however, data collection about transportation can begin. Four categories of data are necessary for the transportation plan:

1. Facts pertaining to the present school transportation system
2. Facts pertaining to the school board transportation policy and the general school operation
3. Facts pertaining to the state transportation policy and procedures
4. Facts pertaining to the community transportation system and the demographics of the community

There is essential information that the planner must have within these four broad headings. Answers to the questions raised in figures 4.1 through 4.4 will provide the planner with those data needed to develop a transportation plan for a desegregated school system.

TABLE 4.6. Building Analysis of Elementary Schools

School	Capacity		Temporary Classroom Capacity	Age		Enrollment				Operating Cost		Energy Cost	
	Total	% Used		Year Built	Years	Current	1970	Change	% Change	Total	Per Unit Capacity	Total	Per Unit Capacity
Eisenhower	675	57.6	4	1952	26	389	740	− 351	− 47%	$36,022	$ 53.36	$ 8,351	$12.37
Eliot	650	72.8	0	1928	50	473	659	− 186	− 28%	38,000	58.46	8,650	13.30
Emerson	800	84.5	0	1976	2	676	574	+ 102	+ 17%	64,914	81.14	24,913	31.14
Eugene Field	600	65.5	0	1922	56	393	309	+ 84	+ 27%	24,540	57.56	11,539	19.23
Franklin	575	54.1	0	1927	51	311	481	− 170	− 35%	30,816	51.36	8,055	14.00
Frost	550	49.8	0	1966	12	274	556	− 282	− 50%	39,435	71.70	9,967	18.12
Fulton	1,000	50.4	4	1961	17	504	999	− 495	− 49%	53,227	53.22	16,569	16.56
Greeley	625	67.2	4	1969	9	420	560	− 140	− 25%	47,752	76.40	19,261	30.81
Grimes	525	67.4	2	1966	12	354	462	− 108	− 23%	48,709	92.77	11,468	21.84
Grissom	925	88.2	8	1969	9	816	423	+ 393	+ 93%	62,234	67.28	28,400	30.70
Hawthorne	700	60.7	8	1952	26	425	903	− 478	− 53%	56,252	56.41	24,947	52.52
Sequoyah	600	47.0	0	1928	50	282	581	− 299	− 51%	30,848	51.41	8,113	13.52
Springdale	725	58.2	6	1925	53	422	673	− 251	− 37%	41,154	56.76	11,501	15.86
Stevenson	475	58.3	0	1966	12	277	381	− 104	− 27%	37,204	78.32	8,828	18.58
Whitman	625	51.8	11	1961	17	324	394	− 70	− 17%	33,905	60.64	8,720	13.95
Whittier	700	46.7	2	1917	61	327	458	− 131	− 28%	40,259	57.51	10,852	15.50
Woods	500	60.4	9	1965	13	302	740	− 438	− 50%	42,632	85.26	15,182	30.36

FIGURE 4.1

Factors Pertaining to the Present School Transportation System

The essential information needed about the current transportation program is

1. How many vehicles are owned by the school system?
2. What number of buses are at present used from some form of contract with outside supplier?
3. What is the age and condition of each vehicle?
4. What has been the board policy on trading of vehicles?
5. What are the load capacities of each of these vehicles?
6. What number of vehicles have been purchased with agreements to maintain them for special use (e.g., handicapped students)?
7. What number of vehicles have been committed to joint usage such as transportation of private school or vocational students?
8. What percentage of the time are these vehicles used for the special purposes referred to in 6 and 7?
9. What has been the annual cost per vehicle for maintenance, fuel, oil, and tires, and insurance?
10. What has been the average number of children per busload and how many trips does each bus make in A.M. and P.M.?
11. What is the number of facilities available for bus maintenance?
12. What are the capacities of these facilities (how many bus bays and how many bays are equipped with lifts, etc.)?
13. What is the petroleum storage capability?
14. What kind of security system is in use to ensure safety of vehicles?
15. What is the number, by category, of maintenance personnel that are at present employed (supervisors, mechanics, mechanic helpers, miscellaneous laborers, etc.)?
16. What number of children at present ride public transportation to school?

It can be seen from figure 4.1 that the data needed about the school transportation system are objective and require no subjective judgment. Each item will have an effect on the kind of judgment that must be made about the purchase, maintenance, fueling, operation, and housing of vehicles.

In figure 4.2, some of the data about the board of education pertains to policies and negotiated contracts. Even though negotiated contracts are in effect, if a school system is under a court order to desegregate, many of these contracts will become inoperable if they conflict with the mandates of the court. Thus the planner must take into consideration board policies and negotiated contracts, but the planner is not necessarily bound to those policies and contracts if they conflict with the wishes of the courts.

FIGURE 4.2

Facts Pertaining to the School Board Transportation
Policy and the General School Operation

The essential information needed about board of education policies is

1. What are the board policies on transportation?
2. What has been the consistency of the maintenance of the policies?
3. What is the negotiated contract with the transportation personnel?

(Continued)

4. What has been the board's purchase procedure for buses (from lowest local bidder, or has it been open regionally or statewide)?
5. What schools are on double sessions?
6. What are the present bell schedules?
7. What number of different bell schedules can reasonably be operated?
8. What are the special programs now in existence that the administration hopes to maintain, and what are the transportation commitments to those programs?
9. What is the policy for supervision on the bus (is driver the sole authority)?

Items 4 and 5 in figure 4.3 are important to the desegregation planner. Item 4 contains the data pertaining to the reimbursement formula used by the state to subsidize the local transportation systems. These formulas vary from state to state but are important because they will significantly affect the amount of expenditures that will be required for transportation by the local school district. The data in item 5 pertain to state averages. These data are important because they allow the desegregation planner to make generalizations about the transportation program even though the local district may not have an extensive history of school transportation.

FIGURE 4.3
Facts Pertaining to the State Transportation Policy and Procedures.

The essential information about state policies and procedures is

1. What are the safety regulations imposed by the state?
2. What are the regulations on the size or capacity of buses?
3. What is the maximum number of students which the State will allow in each bus per load?
4. What is the state formula for reimbursement on transportation? Concerns:
   a. percent of bus cost—maximum
   b. allowances for automatic transmissions, two-way radios, mobile page P.A. systems
   c. reimbursement formula for maintenance, fuel, tires, insurance
   d. reimbursement formulas for per mile driven
   e. any additional state reimbursements for special categories
5. What are the state averages for transportation? Such as
   a. cost per student in board-owned buses, contracted, public, other
   b. number of students transported per bus, per day
   c. cost per bus per year
   d. maintenance, fuel, tires, tubes, and insurance cost per bus per year
   e. number of miles driven per bus per day
   f. number of miles driven per bus per year
6. What is the state program for training bus drivers?

The information about the community is both economic and geographic. It is essential for the desegregation planner to know the natural barriers of rivers, limited-access highways, mountain ranges, canals, and so forth. Any of these physical features in the community can have a significant impact on a desegregation plan. Two points that look relatively close together on a map may be several miles apart because of a canal without access, or a cemetery or an airport. The planner must be aware of these features and must take them into consideration when determining transportation needs. A second factor is the extent of accessibility the school system has to the public transportation system of the community. In most instances, though the community has a public transportation system, it is difficult to achieve the necessary cooperation and accommodation called for in a desegregation plan. Even with these limitations noted, the planner must investigate what the community can provide.

FIGURE 4.4

Facts Pertaining to the Community Transportation System
and the Demographics of the Community.

The essential information about the community that will affect the transportation plan is

1. What are the major arteries for transportation and do they provide access in all directions?
2. What are the remote areas which are difficult to reach?
3. What are the long-range highway department's construction or repair plans on the streets within the district?
4. What are the natural or geographic barriers to transportation?
5. What is the present and projected availability of the public transportation system?
6. What is the present and projected unit price for the public transportation system (cost per bus, per day or cost per hour, or cost per student, per day, or major restrictions such as length of contract, or number of times a day a student may ride, etc.)?
7. What are the state and federal regulations the public transportation system must abide by (bidding, demand on buses, etc.)?
8. What areas in the district does the public transportation system cover and with what level of service?
9. What modifications do the vehicles in the public transportation system need to meet safety regulations imposed by state? (Who will pay for alterations?)
10. What is the local and regional bus contracting potential and do the vehicles meet state safety regulations?
11. What is the present and projected cost per unit (per day, per hour, per year)?
12. What local or regional dealers would be interested in bidding on buses?
13. What are the dealers' estimated bid figures on a specified unit as well as the estimated bid prices on each specified option?
14. What is the estimated time from placement of order to delivery to the district? (This estimate must be as accurate as possible.)
15. What space is available in the district for storage and maintenance of buses? (The board may own property, which could be converted.)
16. What are the contractors' estimated bid prices and construction time for construction of facilities for bus maintenance, repair, and storage?
17. What are the cost of and approximate delivery dates of gasoline tank, truck hand-held radio units, central or base radio units, tow and wrecker truck units, and telephone system?

DEMOGRAPHIC STUDIES

There generally is a constant flow of tudies in urban school systems. These studies address specific problems or areas of the school system that the school board, central administration, or state authorities feel need attention within the school system. Many times, these studies contain useful information for the school desegregation planner. The studies could pertain to facilities and facility utilization, transportation potential and analyses of the community, discipline within the school system, new programs or curriculums within the schools, or a multitude of other items that on the surface may not seem to be directly related to the desegregation plan development.

The planner should collect all such studies that have been produced within the school system over the past five to seven years. The data may not have the currency needed for the desegregation plan, but data can be updated if the items presented in the studies are germane to the needs of the desegregation plan being developed.

SPECIAL PROGRAMS

The location and nature of all special programs conducted in the school system must be identified by the desegregation planner. Programs for children who are blind, deaf, or severely physically or mentally handicapped will usually fall outside the demands of the court-ordered desegregation plan. Even so, these programs must be identified and must be explained in detail so that the court is apprised of the fact that the programs exist and that the special nature of the population served require them to continue to exist.

Other programs also will be affected by the desegregation plan, and these programs must be accounted for by the desegregation planner. Programs such as Title I may be altered as school populations are altered. These alterations could require some shifting of funds or the acquisition of additional funds as schools populations change. Bilingual programs and programs of a like nature must be maintained because they are designed for groups of students with specific needs. Therefore, as student populations are reassigned, the planner must be aware of these programs so that the programs can be moved with the targeted population. A section of each desegregation plan should be devoted to programming.

COMMUNITY INPUT

The desegregation planner must be in contact with the various community groups that exist within the school system. The planner cannot focus on one group with specific needs or desires. The planner must meet with community, business, religious and racial groups, and with any other identifiable parties whose children will be directly affected by the desegregation plan. This does not mean that the desegregator must spend time with every splinter or extremist group within the community. But the desegregator must have input from those groups who make decisions in the community or influence decisions made in the community. When plans are written in isolation from the community, the seeds for failure in implementation are well planted. Information and insights from these groups can be obtained through community meetings, scheduled appointments, or position papers written and presented to the desegregator.

A variety of data must be collected prior to the development of a desegregation plan. Desegregation plans are built on both hard and soft information. Pupil counts, teacher counts, building costs, and transportation information are all hard data that can be computed and put in table form. The soft data of community input, program needs, community changes, and potential of underused buildings are less easily recorded but are nonetheless important to the overall development of the plan.

The citizen whose children will be affected by the implementation of the plan must be able to read the plan and know that the planner actively sought information and then objectively utilized that information in construction of the desegregation plan. Data must be carefully gathered. Accuracy must be maintained through a series of checks and through a series of carefully constructed tables.

SELECTED COURT DECISIONS

Green v. *County School Board,* 391 U.S. 430 (1966).

Hills v. *Gautreaux* (Ill.), 96 S.Ct. 1538 (1976).

Penick v. *Columbus Board of Education* (Ohio D.C.), 429, F.Supp. 229 (1977).

Reed v. *Rhodes,* 422 F.Supp. 708, 790 (N.D. Ohio 1976).

United States v *Scotland Neck City Board of Education,* 92 S.Ct. 2214, 407 U.S. 484, 33 L.Ed.2d 75 (1975).

SELECTED BIBLIOGRAPHY

Forehand, G. A.; M. Ragosta; and D. A. Rock. *Conditions and Processes of Effective School Desegregation.* Princeton, N. J.: Educational Testing Service, 1976.

Foster, Gordon, "Desegregating Urban Schools: A Review of Techniques." *Harvard Educational Review* 43, no. 1 (February 1973): 5–36.

Simpson, Robert J., and William M. Gordon, "School Desegregation: Is Busing for U.S.?" *NOLPE School Law Journal* 3, no. 1 (Spring 1973): 27–36.

5

Techniques for Desegregating a School District

Whether desegregation occurs by court order or voluntary action, the task of formulating an effective desegregation plan is immense. Because of the overall effect on the community, correcting educational inequities often caused by neighborhood housing patterns is a chore far exceeding simple readjustment of numbers and kinds of students attending specific schools in a district. Nevertheless, certain techniques are basic to the task and must be employed early to ensure a plan that will sustain rational inquiry. This chapter examines the nature of these basic techniques.

As noted in the previous chapter, a desegregation plan requires an accurate body of data depicting the racial makeup of the student populations, as well as the current attendance boundaries for the elementary, junior high, and senior high schools. There is also a need for information concerning the location of transportation arteries, rivers, railroad tracks, superhighways, and other physical features that could impinge upon the assignment of students to a specific school or the combining of specific neighborhoods.

In addition, each city has unique features and population patterns that will cause special problems to the desegregation planner. These features must be considered in planning, but convenience cannot take precedence over the requirement that the schools of a community be nonracially identifiable.

Factors in Pupil Assignment

The most desirable assignment patterns are ones that keep distances that must be traveled to and from school to a minimum; the least desirable require extensive travel in either time or distance, the controlling factor being time. However, it must be pointed out that though long distances and extensive travel time are undesirable, the decision in *Swann*[1] established clearly that the issue is *desegregation* and that any technique can and should be employed to eliminate racially identifiable schools.

Aside from the matter of distance to school, three other considerations exist when assigning students for the purpose of desegregation: (1) the burden of the desegregation must not fall disproportionately on one race or economic level; (2) once desegregated, each school must have a racial ratio that reflects the overall racial ratio of the school district;[2] and (3) the number of students assigned to any building must not exceed the established building capacity.

Techniques for Pupil Assignment

Six commonly used pupil-assignment techniques have been successfully employed: rezoning, contiguous pairing, noncontiguous pairing, clustering, single-grade centers, and islands. These techniques are discussed in this chapter in the order of ease and economy of implementation.

REZONING

Most systems offer little freedom of choice regarding where a student goes to school. Students are assigned to specific school attendance zones by residence. School systems found by the courts to be segregated will have attendance zones made up of student populations that are significantly disproportionate to the racial make up of the total community. In many instances the simple redrawing of the school attendance boundaries can have the effect of racially balancing the population. Plate *A* of figure 5.1 is an example of a school attendance boundary in which the racial population of the school does not reflect the racial population of the district.

As shown in plate *B* of figure 5.1, redrawing the attendance boundaries of the school can alter the racial composition of the population of the school. The new school attendance zone would approximate the black-nonblack ratio of the community, which makes the school nonracially identifiable.

Redrawing attendance boundaries causes minimal disruption within the school community and achieves the desired goal of racial balance. This technique is easier to use with high schools because high school attendance zones draw from a larger geographic area. This is the first technique that should be considered when preparing a desegregation plan.

CONTIGUOUS PAIRING

Contiguous attendance zones occur when two adjacent attendance areas share a common boundary. Contiguous pairing can be used when the two attendance areas, viewed alone, have racially identifiable populations, but by combining the populations of the two areas, the result approximates the racial composition of the school system.

FIGURE 5.1
School Attendance Zones

Plate A Before Rezoning

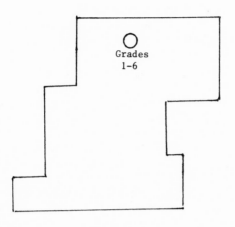

Grades
1-6

Plate B After Rezoning*

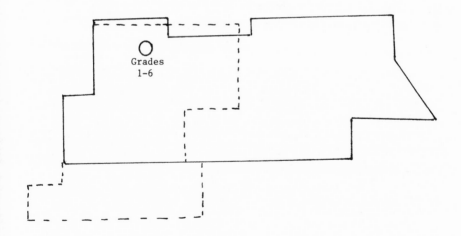

Grades
1-6

* Dotted line depicts outline of original school zone.

Plate *A* of figure 5.2 shows the attendance areas of two schools. Each school is a racially identifiable school; one school is identifiably black and the other identifiably white. Plate *B* of figure 5.2 shows the two school attendance zones with the elimination of the common boundary line. The students of the combined school attendance area are now considered as a single population. The schools are then reorganized, one school to house grades 1, 2, 3 and the other to house grades 4, 5, 6. All students of the combined attendance area who are in the first three grades will attend one school and all students in the combined area who are in grades 4, 5, 6 will attend the other school. Thus, by combining two contiguous attendance zones and changing the grade configurations of two schools, both schools become desegregated and reflect the combined racial composition of the two zones. If the racial composition of the combined zones approximates the racial composition of the total school population, the two schools can be considered nonracially identifiable.

NONCONTIGUOUS PAIRING

In noncontiguous pairing, school attendance areas that do not share a common boundary are combined because the two school populations, put together, will approximate the racial ratio of the school community. In a noncontiguous pairing all students from the identified zones attend certain grades in each school, as in contiguous pairing.

Plate *A* of figure 5.3 shows the attendance zones of two schools. Each school is a racially identifiable school; one school is identifiably black and the other identifiably white. Plate *B* of figure 5.3 shows the two attendance zones after they have been paired. When the student populations of the two zones are combined, all students of the two zones who are in grades, 1, 2, 3 will be assigned to one school, and all students in grades 4, 5, 6 will be assigned to the other school. By bringing together the populations of the attendance zones, each school will reflect the combined racial balance of the two zones and therefore the racial balance of the total school population of the community. With the pupil assignment depicted in plate *B*, all students in the first three grades will attend one school, and all students in grades 4, 5, 6 will attend the other school.

Needed Transportation

Because the two school attendance zones in figure 5.3 do not have a common boundary, transportation will probably be required. The required transportation can be provided in one of two ways. The first way has the students report to the school closest to their home. They are picked up at that site and transported to the alternate site where they receive instruction for the full day. Once the instruction is completed, the students are transported back to the original school site where they proceed on their own to their homes. The

FIGURE 5.2
Contiguous Attendance Areas

Plate A   Contiguous attendance areas, each racially identifiable

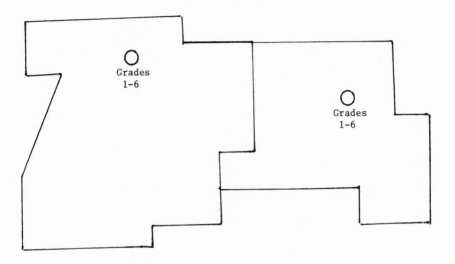

Plate B   Contiguously paired attendance area with two school facilities

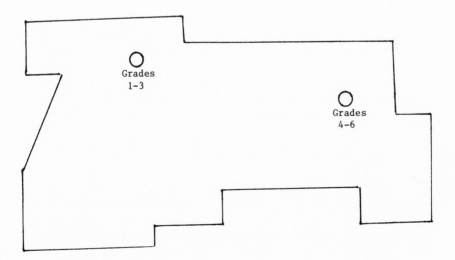

FIGURE 5.3
Noncontiguous Attendance Areas

Plate A   Noncontiguous attendance areas, each racially identifiable

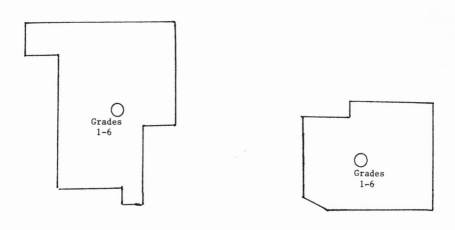

Plate B   Noncontiguous attendance areas with student populations
mixed and each school's grade paired

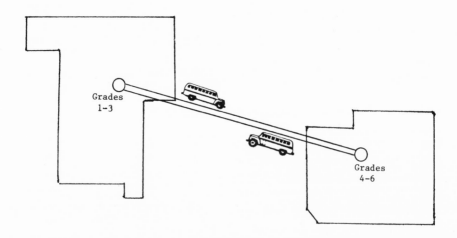

second way is to run a regular school bus route in each zone to pick up students and transport them to the noncontiguous school site. Once the school day is completed, the students are returned to their homes following the same bus route. There are obvious economies in site-to-site transportation.

CLUSTERING

Clustering involves combining more than two school attendance zones. Clustering can take several forms. Plate *A* of figure 5.4 shows three attendance zones. Two of the elementary schools are racially identifiable as nonblack, and one school is racially identifiable as black. By combining the populations of all three elementary schools, a racial balance that approximates the racial makeup of the total school district can be achieved. Plate *B* of figure 5.4 shows the clustering of the three schools. Two schools now have grades 1 through 4, and one school has grades 5 and 6. All fifth and sixth graders from the attendance areas will attend the same school. The attendance zone with the fifth- and sixth-grade school will be split, and students in grades 1 through 4 who live in section *A* will be assigned to one school while students in grades 1 through 4 who live in section *B* will be assigned to the other school.

The three schools, once clustered, will reflect the racial population of the total school community. This arrangement will also necessitate the transportation of students if there are noncontiguous attendance zones in the cluster.

Plate *A* of figure 5.5 shows the same configuration of schools, as that shown in plate *A* of figure 5.4. In this example, one school will house grades 1 and 2, one school will house grades 3 and 4, and the third school will house grades 5 and 6. With this configuration, all students in the three attendance zones who are in first and second grades will attend one school, all in third and fourth grades will attend the second school, and all in fifth and sixth grades will attend the third school.

Thus the three schools depicted in figure 5.5 will be desegregated by making each school within the cluster a two-grade unit. Engaging in this kind of clustering will result in each student's being out of the "home" attendance area four of the six elementary school years. It should also be pointed out that the grade configurations need not be two-grade units. There could be a single-grade center or any other combination of grades depending on the capacity of the buildings and the educational program desired.

When examining the many alternatives available in clustering, it is usually desirable to cluster in such a fashion that students attend only two different schools during the elementary years. This means that in a normal grade arrangement of elementary, junior high, and high school, the student would go to four different school buildings instead of the more traditional three.

FIGURE 5.4
Clustering School Attendance Areas

Plate A Three school attendance areas, each having racially identifiable populations

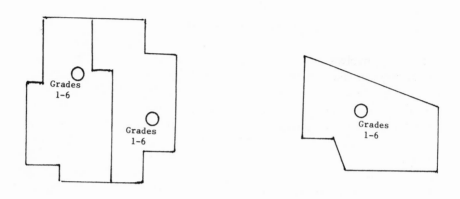

Plate B Three school attendance areas after the pupil
populations have been clustered

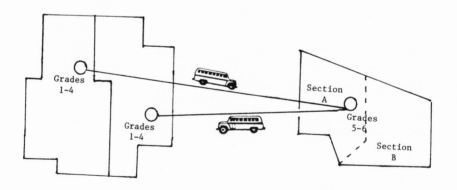

FIGURE 5.5
Clustering and Reconstituting Grades

Plate A   Three school attendance areas, each having racially identifiable populations

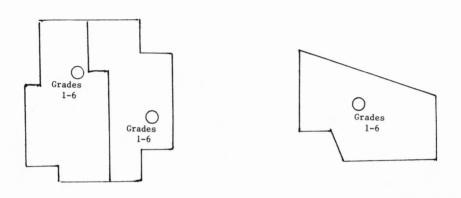

Plate B   Three school attendance areas after clustering and reconstituting the grade arrangements of each school

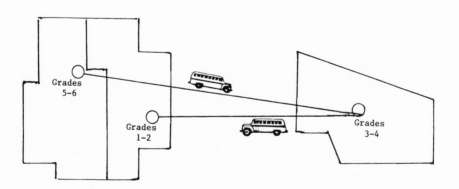

SINGLE-GRADE CENTERS

A variation on clustering is the single-grade center. Plate *A* of figure 5.6 shows four elementary school attendance zones that could be clustered about a single-grade center. Plate *B* of the figure shows that with the establishment of a single sixth-grade center at one school and the conversion of the other schools to grades 1 through 5, the cluster will be desegregated. Thus, all sixth graders in the clustered attendance zone will attend one school while first through fifth graders in the attendance area will be divided among sections *A, B,* and *C* and assigned to the other three attendance areas. A sixth-grade center (or any single-grade center) can be established and a program for the special needs of the preadolescent sixth graders designed and implemented.

The clustering configuration has some appeal for elementary or junior high school students, but if the planner is not careful, the technique could impose a disproportionate responsibility for the desegregation on one racial group.

ISLANDS

There are occasions in preparing desegregation plans when school buildings will be taken out of regular service. Taking a building out of service might happen because of obsolescence or because the building has been designated for alternative use (e.g., as a magnet school or a special-focus center). When a school is taken out of service, students who live in the former attendance area must be reassigned. The reassignment can be achieved in several ways, but the most common way is through islands.

Plate *B* of figure 5.7 shows how the attendance area can be divided with each of the sub-attendance areas reassigned to receiving schools either contiguously or noncontiguously. Students living in the areas will be assigned to new school settings where their presence will improve the racial balance so that the schools will more closely approximate the racial balance of the school community.

The foregoing techniques can be employed to desegregate any school community. Although no one technique can be used universally, a planner should attempt to progress through these techniques in the order presented because the order moves from the more simple to the more complex.

Rezoning has proved to be the most effective means of school desegregation, though contiguous pairing has been received with a minimum amount of criticism. Islands have proved to be the least acceptable form of school desegregation, and of course any form of noncontiguous pairing that requires transportation can become a political as well as a social point of public controversy and debate. Nevertheless, such techniques are often the only reasonable option. It is a rare community that does not require a combination of some, if not all, of these desegregation strategies.

FIGURE 5.6
Single-Grade Center

Plate A   Four school attendance areas, each having racially identifiable school populations

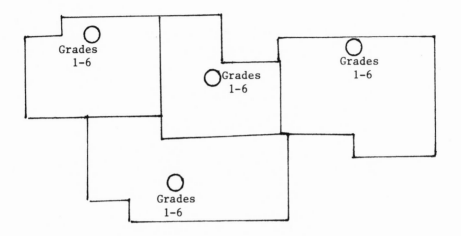

Plate B   Four school attendance areas clustered with a single-grade center

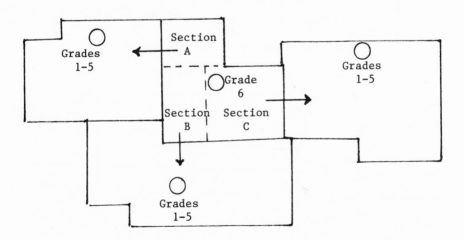

FIGURE 5.7
Islands

Plate A   A racially identifiable attendance area where the building
will be taken out of service

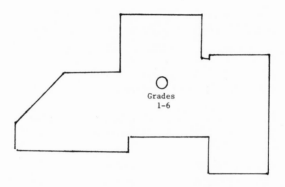

Plate B   School taken out of service with old attendance area divided into islands

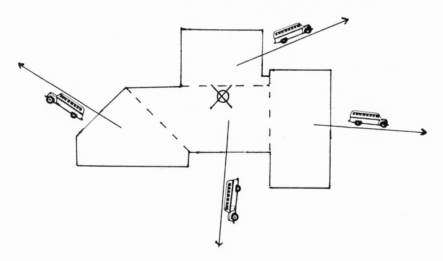

SELECTED COURT DECISIONS

Bradley v. *School Board City of Richmond,* 382 U.S. 103, 86 S.Ct. 224, 15 L.Ed.2d 187 (1965) 338 F.Supp. 67, 184–86 (1972).

Cisneros v. *Corpus Christi Independent School District,* 467 F.2d 142 (1972).

Clemons v. *Board of Education,* 350 U.S. 1006 (Ohio 1956)

Davis v. *Board of School Commissioners of Mobile County,* (Ala.), 91 S.Ct. 1289, 402 U.S. 33, 28 L.Ed.2d 577 (1971).

Spangler v. *Board of Education,* 311 F.Supp. 501 (Calif. 1971).

SELECTED BIBLIOGRAPHY

Computer Assisted Assignment of Students to Schools to Achieve Desegregation. Chicago: Illinois Institute of Technology Research Institute, 1975. 15 pages (pamphlet).

Kalodner, Howard I., and James J. Fishman. *Limits of Justice: The Courts Role in School Desegregation.* Cambridge, Mass.: Ballinger, 1976. 600 pages.

Levinson, Florence H., and Benjamin D. Wright, ed. "School Desegregation: Shadow and Substance." *School Review,* May 1976. 210 pages.

"Research Review of Equal Education, The Status of Desegregation in American Cities: Implication for the State Role." *Research Review of Equal Education* 4 (Fall 1977).

NOTES

1. *Swann* v. *Charlotte-Mecklinburg Board of Education,* 402 U.S. 1 (1970).

2. The ratio need not be exact. A plus or minus factor of 10 to 15 percent is most frequently applied and is usually permissible.

6

Development of the Plan
for Pupil Assignment

Once it is determined that a school system must desegregate, it becomes important for the planner to establish a sequential approach based on carefully collected and accurate data. The data necessary for development of a desegregation plan have been discussed in chapter 4, and the mechanics of desegregation was the subject of chapter 5.

If desegregation is occurring because of litigation, the plan, once prepared and submitted, becomes a document of the courts, and must be able to withstand court scrutiny. But whether the desegregation is court ordered or voluntary, mistakes in addition, tables that do not agree, and information that is inaccurate or inconsistent will create confusion and will weaken the acceptance of even a well-conceived plan.

Court requirements are stated in a desegregation order and establish the extent of remedy desired plus the tolerances that will be considered acceptable. Most court orders are straightforward. The court asks that the school system, or a portion of the school system, be brought into racial balance. Frequently, inexperienced planners attempt to define a court order narrowly, to deal with limited, specific meanings of words, or flatly refuse to acknowledge the spirit of the order. The net result of preparing a plan based on these assumptions is to antagonize the court and protract the inevitable desegregation into a long and costly exercise. Following this course of action will cause local citizens to react negatively, splinter groups to develop and campaign for their particular points of view, and great amounts of dissension, confusion, and frustration within the community at large. When this happens, the ultimate success of the plan may be significantly impaired.

Therefore, the planner must approach the task of designing a desegregation plan with dispassion. The planner must deal with the realities of the data provided and must proceed in a systematic way that meets the spirit as well as the letter of the court order.

COMMUNITY DEMOGRAPHICS

An important part of a desegregation plan is a demographic study of the community. This study should extend back at least ten years in the community's history and should chart the movement of population within the school district. The study should show which neighborhoods have remained racially stable, which have changed from a majority of one race to a majority of another, and which are in an apparent state of transition.

The demographic analysis of a community must focus upon groups of people who share certain selected characteristics, the most common being age, race, and ethnic background. This analysis also should focus on the size and location of groups within the community.

Migrations into or out of neighborhoods are the principle component of demographic change. Charting these migrations can pose some difficult problems because no official agency records are maintained for residential movement. A few agencies and businesses (e.g., the U.S. Postal Service, utilities, and election boards) do maintain some useful records, and data from these sources should be considered. Data from the Chamber of Commerce, real estate groups, industrial commissions, and the like are less reliable, but should be examined. Chamber of Commerce data, for example, tend to be eternally optimistic.

The city or county planning department will be able to supply information concerning those areas of the city that are blighted, deteriorating, or contain many buildings that are structurally obsolete. Further important information for a planner to gain is a description of the density of the population by sections of the school district. Many cities, especially those in the industrial North, are declining in population. These declines frequently result in the abandonment or vacating of large areas of the community that formerly provided enrollment for neighborhood schools.

The planner must also study in some detail the physical features of the community that could influence the desegregation of the schools. Geographic features such as rivers, highways, and lakes are obvious features that must be considered. Less obvious are industrial areas with few children but heavy traffic over bridges and roads that are congested during certain hours of the day, limited-access highways that cut across neighborhoods and divide communities, and large nonresidential areas like airports, cemeteries, parks, and incorporated areas. These features of a city are unique, and they are all possible impediments to the reassignment or transportation of students.

The demographic report is a detailed study of the commmunity, but it should not be a lengthy document that extols the history and virtues of the community. In short, it should be analytical but not epic.

PROFILE OF PUPIL POPULATION

Once the demographics of the community have been examined, an accurate and detailed profile of the pupil population must be drawn. It is essential for the planner to establish a specific date for a census of the student population. In most states this date is sometime in early October of the school year. At that time a school system must make an official report to the state's department of education of the pupil count by race, grade, sex, and school. If the official data reported to the state are not adequate, the annual report required by the Office of Civil Rights of the Department of Health, Education, and Welfare can be used. This information consists of a racial-ethnic breakdown, by school, of the school system.

Ethnic Composition of the School System

A table reflecting the ethnic composition of the schools for the past seven to ten years should be constructed. This and all subsequent tables must use data from a specific official source, (e.g., Office of Civil Rights or the official state report data). Whichever data are used should be used consistently. Basic data sources should not be mixed.

Information presented in the table constructed from these data will show school population trends and indicate to the planner the possibilities of excess classroom capacities or limited classroom capacities. Table 6.1 is an example of an ethnic composition table. Coupled with the community demographic data, this information will help the planner establish a basis for projecting population growth or decline for subsequent years.

TABLE 6.1. Ethnic Composition of the Regular Public School Student Population, Seven-Year Comparison, 1974–80

		Black		American Indian		Asian American		Hispanic		White	
Year	Total	No.	%	No.	%	No.	%	No.	%	No.	%
1974	150,707	86,371	57.31	279	.19	197	.13	2,520	1.67	61,340	40.70
1975	146,048	85,291	56.95	304	.21	204	.14	2,890	1.93	59,554	40.77
1976	142,404	81,318	57.17	310	.22	234	.17	2,795	1.96	57,647	40.48
1977	137,572	79,027	57.45	349	.25	307	.22	3,106	2.26	54,783	39.82
1978	132,029	75,789	57.40	247	.32	344	.26	3,492	2.65	51,977	39.37
1979	128,154	73,706	57.51	335	.26	357	.28	3,691	2.88	50,065	39.07
1980	122,706	71,797	58.51	479	.39	377	.30	3,670	2.99	46,383	37.80

DATA SOURCE: *Office of Civil Rights Reports*, 1974, 1975, 1976, 1977, 1978, 1979, 1980.

Once the seven- to ten-year comparison has been constructed, a table showing the current student population should be developed, even though this table may duplicate data in the first table. This second table should present the current student population subject to the court order and the desegregation plan being drawn. This table should also establish racial percentages that will form the basis for desegregation judgments to be made throughout the entire plan. Table 6.2 depicts an example of the racial composition of one school system.

TABLE 6.2. Ethnic Composition of the Regular Public School Student Population, October 1980

Ethnic Group	Number	Percent of Student Population
American Indian/Alaska Native	479	.4
Asian/Pacific Islander	377	.3
Hispanic	3,670	2.9
Black	71,797	58.6
White	46,383	37.8
TOTAL	122,706	100.0

DATA SOURCE: *Office of Civil Rights Report,* October 1980.

Analysis of School Population by Race and Grade Level

Following the presentation of the racial composition of the total school system, there needs to be a summary of the total school population by race and grade level. This information is necessary in helping the planner locate any variations in student populations that must be accounted for. It also indicates to the planner if the school population is changing racially or remaining stable. Table 6.3 depicts a summary table.

TABLE 6.3. Current School Population, by Grade or Program, October 1980

Grade or Program	Adult Ed. Center	Night School	Technical Branch Night	Regular Programs	Total
Pre K				1,685	1,685
K				9,849	9,849
1				10,322	10,322
2				8,652	8,652
3				8,231	8,231
4				8,273	8,273
5				8,388	8,388
6				8,600	8,600
7				9,292	9,292
8				9,073	9,073
9	106	105	10	9,336	9,557
10	410	191	19	10,418	11,038
11	476	294	28	9,019	9,817
12	299	300	62	6,888	7,549
Ungraded		12	116	206	334
EMR					
elementary				2,519	2,519
secondary			50	1,948	1,998
special					
Postgraduate		69	34	7	110
TOTAL	1,291	971	319	122,706	125,287

DATA SOURCE: *Office of Civil Rights Report,* October 1980, for regular program; *State Pupil Population Report,* October 1980, for special programs.

In table 6.3 a planner should note the significant dip in the student populations of grades 5 and 6. This decline will have an impact as those students move through their school years. Also, the planner should note the significant increase in first- and second-grade students, more notable in the second grade. Additionally, there seems to be a significant drop in enrollment between tenth and twelfth grades.

Analysis of School Organizational Patterns

Following an analysis of the school population by grade, it becomes necessary to examine the student population by grade in each building and the racial ratio of the building. The most efficient way to make this analysis is to separate the various school units with respect to organizational patterns that dominate within the community. Generally, large school systems are divided into elementary, junior high, and high school educational units. At times the grade placement per building does not follow the exact kindergarten through grade 6 elementary, grades 7 through 9 junior high, and grades 10 through 12 high school. But even irregular grade placements can be determined, and the population should be reported in that manner. Figure 6.1 analyzes grade patterns in the elementary schools of a city being desegregated.

FIGURE 6.1

Analysis of Elementary School Grade Patterns in a Prototypic School District

There are 84 elementary schools. With a few exceptions, they contain grades 1 through 6. Most have kindergartens and special education classes.

The elementary schools in the system that do *not* have kindergarten (K) through 6 or 1 through 6 configurations are

Mark Twain K through 4

Mary McCloud 4 through 6, and EMR

Murray Franklin K through 8

Rosepatch K through 3, and EMR

Thomas Long K through 4

Williams Holmes K through 4

In the analysis presented in figure 6.1 the common elementary school configuration for the school system is grades 1 through 6 with many schools having kindergarten. But six schools within the system are exceptions. These schools could cause special problems when the planner draws the desegregation plan. Thus they must be visited and given special study.

Detailed Individual School Analysis

Following a general analysis of the elementary schools (see figure 6.1), detailed by school and grade, analysis of each of the system's elementary schools must be made. Table 6.4 is a sample of the kind of table that should be constructed for this analysis.

For a school system with a large number of school buildings, the detailed analysis table will be several pages long. Because of this, schools should be listed in alphabetical order by organizational type (e.g., elementary, middle or junior high, high school), or whatever is the organizational arrangement by level in the particular school district. Note that each school's capacity, the grades it houses, its total population, its total black population, its nonblack population, and the percentage of its black population are all indicated in table 6.4. There is an implicit assumption that the racial balance of the school will be generally spread evenly throughout the grades (e.g., if the school is 75 percent black and 25 percent white, each grade of the school will probably approximate this ratio).

After analyzing the school system on a school, grade, and race basis, summarizing statements of the distribution of elementary students should be made. These summarizing statements should be demographic in nature so that the planner has a clear understanding of the task ahead. Figure 6.2 is a sample of a good summary statement.

FIGURE 6.2
Summarizing Statement: Distribution of Elementary School Students

An analysis of the data presented reveals that 80 schools have 95% or greater black student population and that 33 have a 95% greater nonblack population, 15 schools have 55% black/45% nonblack ratios of the school population.

Sunbeam and Alexander Graham Bell schools, appearing in this table are special schools (blind and hard of hearing) and are reported simply to make a complete accounting for all students in the school district. The two schools will not be a part of the desegregation plan because children who attend the schools have special physical handicaps that require special learning settings.

As one can see, the summary statement identifies the extent of the problem that must be resolved. The statement also informs the courts and the public that two schools are being excluded from the desegregation plan because of the schools' special nature.[1]

Following the demographic analysis of the elementary schools, a similar demographic analysis must be made of the junior high and high schools. Tables 6.5 and 6.6 have been constructed in order to give a proper demographic picture of the racial composition of the secondary schools of the system.

Once this information has been assembled, and each school has been reported with respect to racial composition, the planner is ready to begin the task of determining how students should be reassigned in accordance with the direction of the court.

MAPPING THE DISTRICT

A critical tool in the development of a desegregation plan for a school system is a set of maps locating each school and its current attendance boundaries. There should be three sets of maps: one to show elementary schools, a

TABLE 6.4. Student Population for the Elementary Schools, October 1980

School	Capacity	Grades								Total	Black	Nonblack	% Black
		EMR	K	1	2	3	4	5	6				
Adlai Stevenson	608	9	71	71	53	63	74	85	80	506	506	0	100
Alfred A. Benesch	715	13	116	127	109	79	92	68	69	715	715	0	100
Almira	828	—	129	109	99	89	94	93	95	708	5	703	.7
Andrew J. Rickoff	678	35	86	96	71	97	90	89	114	678	678	0	100
Anthony Wayne	670	6	190	118	119	72	93	83	70	670	651	19	97.2
William C. Bryant	452	29	72	49	51	52	40	53	64	410	0	410	0
William H. Brett	461	45	76	68	38	40	51	42	38	398	18	380	4.5
William H. McGuffey	369	—	51	62	50	39	92	—	—	320	195	125	60.9
William R. Harper	370	8	39	45	34	36	36	44	39	281	0	281	0
Willow	358	10	42	55	31	35	34	33	45	285	5	280	1.8
TOTALS		2,519	11,534	10,322	8,652	8,231	8,273	8,388	8,621	66,608	38,677	27,931	58.07

DATA SOURCE: *State Pupil Population Report*, October 1980. Capacity figures: *Local Board Building Report*, May 1977.

TABLE 6.5. Student Population for the Junior High Schools, October 1980

School	Capacity	EMR	Grades			Total	Black	Nonblack	% Black
			7	8	9				
A. B. Hart	1,680	58	389	386	464	1,297	367	930	28.3
Addison	2,100	28	266	287	266	847	844	3	99.7
Alexander Hamilton	1,408	34	362	347	394	1,137	1,136	1	99.9
Audubon	2,418	76	458	448	491	1,472	1,464	9	99.5
Carl F. Shuler	1,490	—	378	337	420	1,135	180	955	15.9
Central	1,932	74	226	256	225	781	776	5	99.4
Charles A. Mooney	2,135	27	390	392	470	1,279	6	1,273	.5
Wilbur Wright	1,925	40	380	383	345	1,148	37	1,111	3.2
William D. Howells	1,225	62	290	250	232	834	148	686	17.7
Willson	1,050	—	187	174	165	526	302	224	57.4
TOTALS		1,079	9,124	8,880	8,598	27,681	16,028	11,653	57.9

DATA SOURCE: *State Pupil Population Report,* October 1980. Capacity figures: *Local Board Building Report,* May 1977.

TABLE 6.6. Student Population for the High Schools, October 1980

School	Capacity	EMR	Grades				Total	Black	Nonblack	% Black
			9	10	11	12				
Collinwood	3,935	68	531	429	354	354	1,736	1,012	724	58.2
East	2,670	126	—	951	398	338	1,813	1,759	54	96.9
East Technical	3,245	—	—	714	810	496	2,020	2,019	1	99.9
Glenville	4,230	121	—	980	713	523	2,337	2,337	—	100
John Marshall	2,395	23	—	450	485	442	1,400	3	1,397	.2
Max S. Hays	15,765	—	—	269	249	216	734	286	448	38.6
Martin L. King	1,570	134	130	169	86	28	853	847	6	99.3
South High	3,085	—	6	652	700	475	1,833	372	1,461	20.3
West Technical	4,165	108	—	1,209	840	667	2,824	17	2,807	.6
TOTALS	45,806	1,075	725	10,418	9,019	6,888	28,431	17,041	11,390	59.94

DATA SOURCE: *State Pupil Population Report,* October 1980. Capacity figures: *Local Board Building Report,* May 1977.

second to show junior high or middle schools, and a third to show high schools. It is essential that the maps be easy to read and that the attendance boundaries be accurate. The three maps should be of the same dimensions. Probably the most effective map presentation is that of a large base map of the school system, a map big enough to show the streets by name and the physical features of the community.

Overlays made from sheets of acetate, cut to the size of the base map, with schools indicated and school boundaries outlined, need to be prepared. A separate acetate overlay should be made for each of the three kinds of school units. Thus the planner, by placing the acetate for elementary schools over the acetate for high schools, can see where and how various attendance boundaries overlap. These overlays make it easier to determine feeder patterns and identify any inconsistencies in pupil assignments.

The importance of a good set of maps cannot be overstated. If the maps available to the planner are not readable, or if the maps do not show with a high degree of precision the current attendance boundaries of the school system, mistakes and misjudgments can be easily made in the development of the final plan.

FACILITY ANALYSIS

The demographic information will show the planner those sections of the city that are experiencing population decline or a general deterioration. A study of the school census data over the past several years will also indicate the growth and stability characteristics of the various sections of the community. If there is a declining school population, and if there are excesses in capacity, then the judicious closing of some schools could facilitate the desegregation of the city.[2] Drops in enrollment result in empty classrooms or, in many instances, overly small classes within buildings. In many urban areas it is possible to close a number of schools as a result of a significant drop in enrollments.

Criteria for Closing Schools

The problem, of course, is which schools to close. Criteria must be developed so that those schools most appropriate for closing can be identified. Care must be taken to avoid closing schools only in black communities or only in nonblack communities. Additionally, some schools often have a special historical significance in the community, and though they might qualify for closing, it would be unwise to close them. The closing of schools in connection with a desegregation plan should be done judiciously, and the community must be made aware that the selection of schools for closing was not done capriciously.

The following are some criteria by which judgments about school closings may be made. These criteria are developed as general statements and would of course have to be modified by the local planner to meet specific needs of the school system.

Declining enrollment. When a school drops substantially below rated capacity (e.g., less than 60 percent or fewer than 300 total students).

Sharpness of decline. When a school has an enrollment decline of greater than 30 percent over a five- to seven-year period.

Cost of operation/energy drain. When a school cannot be operated economically due to heating plant, maintenance cost, etc. A formula for energy utilization would be to divide the total building *capacity* by the cubic feet of natural gas used (or gallons of oil used, or tons of coal used). This will give up energy consumption per unit of capacity figure.

Age of buildings. When a building reaches the point that the cost of maintenance and/or remodeling are excessively high. Buildings fifty years or older generally fall in this category.

Urban change. When a building location becomes inaccessible, undesirable, or hazardous, due to urban deterioration, urban development/renewal, or alterations of traffic routes.

Conversion/recycling potential. When a building location or associated features provide good prospects for sale or conversion to other uses.

Desegregative impact. When the closing of a building and subsequent consolidation/redistricting can improve the racial balance.

All or some of these criteria can be used to determine which school buildings should be taken out of service. Before the final judgment is made to close, a building should satisfy several criteria. In other words, before a building is recommended for closing it should be established beyond a doubt that the building is no longer desirable as an educational facility.

PUPIL ASSIGNMENT

Once the demographic data pertaining to the school community have been generated, and once judgments have been made pertaining to the closing of selected buildings within the school system, the planner is ready to begin the task of student reassignment. Reassigning students must be done in such a manner that the burden of the desegregation does not fall disproportionately on one racial or economic group within the community. Therefore, in order to avoid making inequitable recommendations for pupil assignments, a set of guidelines for pupil assignment must be established.[3] The following are some common guidelines agreed upon by courts and experienced planners.

Black/nonblack ratio. When the black/nonblack ratio of the community is such that the nonblack ratio is greater than 35 percent, then a school building is deemed desegregated if the student population has a racial balance, that is, is within 15 percent of the systemwide black/nonblack ratio.[4]

Preschool children. Kindergarten and prekindergarten students are generally not included in desegregation plans because the typical kindergarten program is half-day and voluntary.

Special programs. Students who are severely mentally retarded, physically handicapped, blind, or deaf are typically provided programs of instruction in special settings. Because of the special instructional needs of these students, and if they are not covered by P.L. 94-142 ("mainstreaming law"), they are typically excluded from desegregation planning.

Locating students. The residence of all students—elementary, junior high/middle, or high school—is determined by the elementary zone in which they live because this zone traditionally is the smallest attendance unit within the school system.[5]

Optional attendance zones. All optional attendance zones within a school system must be eliminated and students in those zones assigned to specific elementary attendance areas. The so-called freedom of choice plans operated in many communities have usually simply served to perpetuate the segregation of that school community.[6]

The foregoing conditions for assignment are the ones most widely agreed to by desegregation planners. Before entering into the desegregation of a community, a statement of *essential conditions* such as this must be established and agreed upon so that the desegregation planning will remain objective and no group will be unduly affected once the plan is developed and implemented.

HIGH SCHOOL FEEDER ATTENDANCE ZONES

In order to provide consistency in the pupil-assignment patterns, all high school boundaries must be redefined so that they include several elementary schools and one or more junior high schools. This redefinition of boundaries must be made so that the elementary attendance areas are totally inside a single high school attendance area. This redefinition must also include one or more junior high schools within the boundary of the high school attendance area. As it develops, using this approach, existing junior high school attendance areas are not factor in desegregation planning and initially need not be considered.

The elementary attendance zone, once defined within a high school attendance zone, becomes the desegregating unit (i.e., students living in the specified elementary zone will remain together throughout their twelve years of schooling). Figure 6.3 is an example that summarizes this approach.

FIGURE 6.3
The Elementary Attendance Zone as the Desegregating Unit

1. Herman G. Brown is the elementary school attendance area.
2. The elementary students of the Herman G. Brown attendance area will be assigned either by rezoning, pairing, or clustering for their elementary years of instruction. The students will remain together as they proceed through the various grades of the elementary school.
3. The junior high school students living in the Herman G. Brown elementary attendance area will go to the James Flannery Junior High School.
4. The high school students living in the Herman G. Brown elementary school attendance area will go to the Lloyd Williams High School.

Thus the child who lives in Herman G. Brown Elementary School attendance area and neighborhood will remain with that school group throughout his twelve-year career.

Additionally, the student, once beginning school, will change schools only four times during the twelve-year tenure if the elementary years are assigned carefully (e.g., the change from the present attendance pattern would be that the student would go to two elementary schools, a junior high school, and a high school). This differs from the currently accepted pattern where the student changes school three times in twelve years.

As one can see from figure 6.3, once students are identified by their elementary attendance zone of residence, the elementary attendance zone becomes the unit for desegregation.

The high school attendance zone is selected because it covers the greatest geographic area and because natural feeder patterns can be developed with normally articulated educational programs provided for the students. In communities with several high schools, the planner should first attempt to redraw the high school attendance boundaries to include complete elementary attendance zones that will provide a racially balanced high school population. Once this is done, it simply becomes a matter of pairing and clustering elementary schools within the high school zone and then assigning students by elementary area to a specific junior high school. Figure 6.4 is an example that describes this process.

FIGURE 6.4
Balancing the Races within the High School Zone

The community to be desegregated has a racial population 40 percent black, 60 percent non-black. By redistricting the Verne Troxel High School attendance area to include the attendance areas of eight elementary schools, the planner can realize a 42 percent black population and 58 percent white population. This balance is well within an acceptable 15 percent variance; thus the Verne Troxel High School attendance area could be considered racially balanced.

Within the high school district the elementary attendance areas must now be balanced. This is done by redistricting, pairing, or clustering. Let us assume that two elementary schools are paired, the Schlarb Elementary School with an 85 percent black population and Mary Morrisey Elementary School with a 100 percent nonblack population. In the pairing scheme, Schlarb will have grades 1 through 3 and Morrisey will have grades 4 through 6. Thus the elementary populations are now racially balanced at each grade level.

The junior high school students living in the Morrisey elementary attendance area and the Schlarb elementary attendance area will attend the Fayak Junior High School. Because when Morrisey and Schlarb students were combined, racial balance was achieved, it is estimated that approximately this same balance will exist for the junior high school students from the two areas. Therefore, by assigning the junior high school students from the two elementary areas to the same junior high school, racial balance will be realized at that level also.

All high school students living in Morrisey and Schlarb elementary attendance areas will attend Verne Troxel High School. Again, because racial balance was created at the elementary level by combining the two districts, racial balance will also occur at the high school level with the combining of the high school students who live in the two elementary districts.

Thus the entire feeder pattern of Verne Troxel High School district is desegregated. More important, the students, once they come together in first grade, will remain together throughout their twelve-year public education career. This allows for articulation of program plus greater permanancy in the relationships that students will establish among themselves.

If it is impossible to redraw a single high school attendance boundary to achieve racial balance, then the next option is to contiguously pair[7] two high school attendance zones. As with the single high school attendance zone, this would mean that a configuration of elementary attendance zones would have to be established so that the overall racial composition of the student bodies would reflect the total racial composition of the school system being desegre-· gated. Once the high school attendance zones were contiguously paired, the same process of desegregation followed in the single high school attendance zone would be implemented (see figure 6.5).

FIGURE 6.5
Contiguous Pairing of High School Attendance Zones

The school system to be desegregated has a 52 percent black population and 48 percent non-black population. After establishing racial balance in the high school attendance areas by redistricting, it is determined that some high school attendance areas cannot be redistricted and balanced. The next step is pairing contiguous high school zones.

It is determined that if Sidner High School and Freels High School are paired contiguously, they will have a combined student population with a racial composition that is 47 percent black and 53 percent nonblack. Combining the populations of these two high school attendance areas establishes a ratio that reflects the community and thus removes the racial identifiability of the two schools. To achieve school-by-school balance in this new attendance area, the process of redistricting, pairing, and assigning in the elementary attendance areas must begin again.

First those elementary districts within the new Sidner/Freels high school attendance area that can be racially balanced by redistricting are identified and boundaries redrawn. Next, those contiguous elementary attendance areas that can be combined in order to achieve racial balance are combined. Finally, those districts that must be noncontiguously paired or clustered are combined.

Stollar Elementary School is 92 percent nonblack. Arthur E. Thomas Elementary School is 96 percent black. By pairing these two schools, a racially balanced population can be achieved in both schools. All children in grades 1 through 3 will attend Stollar Elementary School and all in grades 4 through 6 will attend the Arthur E. Thomas Elementary School. These two elementary schools are now racially balanced.

There are four junior high schools in the newly constituted Sidner/Freels high school attendance area; even so, the junior high school students who live in the Thomas and Stollar elementary attendance areas will be assigned to only one junior high school, the Robert J. Simpson Junior High School. Likewise, all high school students living in the Stollar and Thomas elementary attendance areas will attend only one high school, the Sidner High School.

Thus students living in the Stollar and Thomas elementary attendance areas will attend four schools during their twelve-year career. They begin at Stollar Elementary, move to Thomas Elementary, then on to Simpson Junior High and finally Sidner High School. This feeder pattern again allows for articulation of program and provides a desegregated feeder system.

A third pattern for the desegregation of high schools in a school district is needed for those high school attendance areas that are still racially identifiable after redistricting and after contiguous pairing. This third pattern would be the pairing of noncontiguous high school attendance areas. It is in this pairing that the greatest amount of transportation must take place, and therefore this technique for desegregating is employed last (see figure 6.6).

The foregoing text and examples incorporate accepted techniques for desegregating a school system. As demonstrated in each example, the key is the establishment of a racially balanced high school attendance area. Once that racial balance has been determined, the elementary schools within the newly redefined high school attendance areas are racially balanced through either redistricting, pairing, or clustering. Note that throughout the process there are no specifically drawn junior high school attendance areas. The junior high schools receive students who are identified through their residence in elementary attendance zones. The assignment of the elementary attendance zones establishes the junior high school populations. In like manner, the elementary attendance areas identify the placement of high school students. Maintaining the feeder approach to desegregation allows the neighborhood of students to remain intact and at the same time provides classrooms that reflect the overall racial balance of the district.

FIGURE 6.6
Noncontiguous Pairing of High School Attendance zones

The community is 45 percent black and 55 percent nonblack. After redistricting some high school attendance areas and contiguously pairing others, the Lawrence Peach and Thomas Franklin high schools are still racially identifiable. By combining the student populations of these two noncontiguous attendance areas, a racial balance of 48 percent black and 52 percent nonblack can be achieved. Thus the two attendance areas, when combined, have a population that is within the acceptable range for nonracial identifiability. Once balance has been determined, the process of combining the elementary attendance zone and identifying the junior high school feeders must proceed as in the previous examples.

By combining the elementary school populations of Sally Page Elementary School, Lowell Owens Elementary School, and Warren Smith Elementary School, a racial balance can be achieved, the Page and Smith elementary schools being racially identifiable as white and the Owens school being racially identifiable as black. Thus a cluster of the three schools is identified. The Page and Smith elementary schools will be redesignated to house grades 1 through 4 while the Owens school will be designated to house grades 5 and 6. With these reassignments fifth and sixth graders from the Page and Smith elementary attendance area will attend the Owens attendance area, and first through fourth graders from the Owens attendance area will be divided between the Page and Smith elementary schools.

All junior high school students living in the Page, Smith, and Owens elementary attendance areas will be assigned to the Richard Devore Junior High School. Likewise, all high school students residing in the Page, Smith, and Owens elementary attendance areas will be assigned to the Thomas Franklin High School.

This completes the feeder process for the noncontiguously paired Peach/Franklin high school attendance area. Consistent with previous patterns, each student will attend four schools in a twelve-year career, and age mates will remain together in an articulated program for the full twelve years.

The following situations are hypothetical instances of pupil assignment using the previously discussed techniques: redistricting, contiguous pairing, and noncontiguous pairing.

A Single High School Attendance District

The racial balance of this school community is 31 percent black and 69 percent nonblack. Using a factor of 15 percent, the schools of the district will be racially nonidentifiable if each school in the district is within a range of 16 percent black/84 percent nonblack to 46 percent black/54 percent nonblack.

Shriver High School will be racially balanced by redefining its attendance area to include six elementary schools and two junior high schools. The six elementary schools that constitute the new Shriver high school district are Lane, Camper, Smiley, McAdams, Selong, and Fitzgerald. The two junior high schools included in the new Shriver high school district are Moss and Harris.

Table 6.7 shows the current student enrollment of the elementary schools that make up the newly constituted Shriver High School. Enrollment figures contained in the table represent current populations and are not the recommended populations.

The total elementary school population shown in Table 6.7 reflects a racial composition of approximately 25 percent black and 75 percent nonblack. It has been established that the overall racial ratio of the community is 31 percent black and 69 percent nonblack; thus this newly constituted

TABLE 6.7. Current Enrollments of Elementary Schools in the Newly Constituted Shriver High School Attendance District

| School | Student Enrollment | | % Black | Total |
	Black	Nonblack		
Elementary Schools				
Lane	141	369	27.0	510
Camper	56	554	9.2	610
Smiley	9	485	1.8	494
McAdams	19	516	3.0	535
Selong	312	150	67.0	462
Fitzgerald	297	346	46.0	643
TOTALS	834	2,420	25.6	3,254

high school attendance district is within an acceptable racial ratio range, although three individual schools are "out of balance."

Table 6.8 contains the projected junior high and high school student populations that reside in the elementary attendance zones of the new Shriver high school district. If the projected populations in table 6.8 remain acccurate, both junior high and high schools in the new Shriver high school attendance area will have an approximate ratio of 25 percent black and 75 percent nonblack, which is within the established racial ratio range. Again, however, it will be noted that some individual schools are not racially balanced. To balance schools within attendance zones, the planner must initiate school pairings.

Table 6.9 contains the elementary school pairings for the Shriver high school attendance area. The reassignments proposed for the Shriver high school attendance area include the redistricting of the Lane elementary attendance area, pairing the Camper/Fitzgerald attendance areas and clustering the Smiley, McAdams, and Selong attendance areas.

Table 6.10 shows the junior high and high school feeder patterns for the Shriver high school attendance area. Any junior high school student living

TABLE 6.8. Projected Junior High and High School Populations, by Elementary Attendance Areas

| Attendance Area | Junior High School | | | | High School | | | |
	B	NB	% B	Total	B	NB	% N	Total
Lane	53	157	25.2	210	54	147	2.6	201
Camper	24	235	9.3	259	23	214	9.7	237
Smiley	3	204	1.4	207	3	185	1.6	188
McAdams	7	220	3.0	227	7	199	3.3	206
Selong	141	65	70.1	206	125	51	71.0	176
Fitzgerald	121	150	44.6	271	120	136	46.8	256
TOTALS	349	1,031	25.2	1,380	332	932	26.2	1,264

TABLE 6.9. Assignments for Elementary Populations of the Shriver High School Attendance Area

School Pair	Proposed Grades	Capacity	Current Populations		Proposed Populations			
			Black	Nonblack	Black	Nonblack	% Black	Totals
Lane	K–6	540	141	369	141	369	27.6	510
Camper	K, 1–3	730	56	554	353	900	28.2	1253
Fitzgerald	K, 4–6	730	297	346				
Smiley	K, 1–4	600	9	458				
McAdams	K, 5, 6	850	19	516	340	1151	22.8	1491
Selong	K, 1–4	480	312	150				

TABLE 6.10. Junior High School Feeder Pattern for the Shriver High School Attendance Area

Junior High: Elementary Feeder Zones	Capacity	Approximate Number Junior High Students		New Population			
		Black	Nonblack	Black	Nonblack	% Black	Total
Moss	1,000						740
Lane		53	157				
Camper		24	235	198	542	26.8	
Fitzgerald		121	150				
Harris	900						640
Smiley		3	204				
McAdams		7	220	151	489	23.6	
Selong		141	65				

High School Feeder Pattern for the Shriver High School Attendance Area

High School: Junior High Feeder Zones	Capacity	Approximate Number High School Students		New Population			
		Black	Nonblack	Black	Nonblack	% Black	Total
Shriver	1,500						1264
Moss		197	497	332	932	26.2	
Harris		135	435				

within the designated elementary attendance areas will attend the junior high school noted in the left-hand column. All high school students living in the six elementary attendance districts will attend Shriver High School.

Figure 6.7 is a mock-up showing the configuration of elementary schools and their relative location to one another. Figure 6.8 is a mock-up showing the configuration of the junior high schools and the relative location of the elementary feeders. High school location is shown in figures 6.7 and 6.8 by a star.

The following is a summary of the feeder pattern established in the redistricted Shriver high school attendance district.

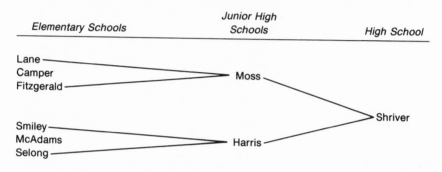

| | Junior High | |
| Elementary Schools | Schools | High School |

within the designated elementary attendance areas will attend the junior

A Multiple High School Attendance District

What follows is an example of desegregating an attendance area with more than one high school. Whether the multiple high school attendance areas are contiguous or noncontiguous is unimportant to the basic approach, although the planner must always be conscious of time and distance when working with noncontiguous areas. The planner would also be well advised to try to limit the mulitple high school areas to two high schools. If more than two high schools are included, the planner may lose the ability to keep student populations in logical feeder patterns.

The school community racial balance for this situation is 37 percent black and 63 percent nonblack. Using a factor of 15 percent, the schools of the district will be racially nonidentifiable if each school in the district is within a range of 22 percent black/78 percent nonblack to 52 percent black/48 percent nonblack.

Clinton and Branch high schools, if paired, will be racially balanced by redefining the attendance areas to include ten elementary schools and three junior high schools. The ten elementary schools that would constitute the new Clinton/Branch high school district are Anderson, Brown, Fritz, Kiffer, Miller, Moses, North, Ridge, Valley, and Williams. The three junior high schools now included in the Clinton/Branch high school district are Dunn, Griffith, and Harwood.

The current student enrollment of elementary schools in the newly constituted Clinton/Branch high school attendance area is shown in table 6.11.

FIGURE 6.7
Elementary Schools as Desegregated in the Shriver
High School Attendance District

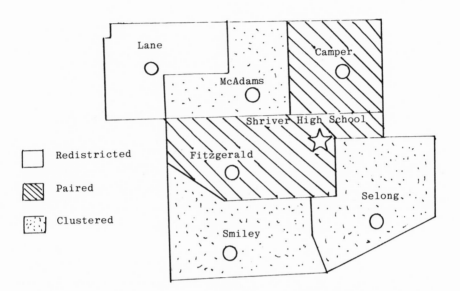

□ Redistricted

▨ Paired

▨ Clustered

FIGURE 6.8
Junior High School Feeders in the Shriver High School Attendance District

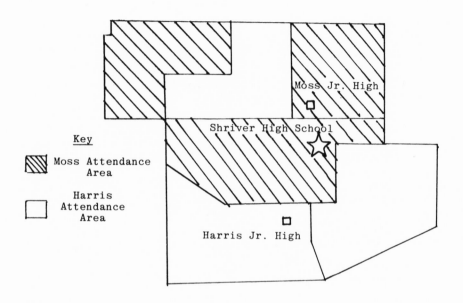

The enrollment figures are of current populations and are not the recommended populations.

The elementary school population shown in table 6.11 reflects a racial composition of approximately 38 percent black, 62 percent nonblack. It has been established that the overall racial ratio of the community is 37 percent black and 63 percent nonblack; thus this newly constituted combined high school district is within an acceptable racial ratio range.

TABLE 6.11. Current Enrollments of the Elementary Schools that Constitute the Clinton-Branch Combined High School District

| School | Student Enrollment | | % Black | Total |
	Black	Nonblack		
Anderson	415	76	84.5	491
Brown	51	427	10.7	478
Fritz	670	270	71.2	940
Kiffer	227	392	36.7	619
Miller	169	310	35.3	479
Moses	532	55	90.6	587
North	42	360	10.4	402
Ridge	10	392	2.5	402
Valley	8	874	.9	882
Williams	9	267	3.3	276
TOTALS	2,133	3,423	38.3	5,556

Table 6.12 contains the projected junior and senior high school student populations that reside in the elementary attendance zones of the newly combined Clinton/Branch high school district. If the projected populations in Table 6.12 remain accurate, the junior and senior high schools in the new Clinton/Branch high school attendance area will have an approximate ratio of 38–40 percent black and 62–60 percent nonblack, which is well within the established racial ratio range.

TABLE 6.12. Projected Junior and Senior High School Populations, by Elementary Attendance Areas

| Attendance Area | Junior High School | | | | Senior High School | | | |
	B	NB	% B	Total	B	NB	% N	Total
Anderson	183	37	83.2	220	181	34	84.2	215
Brown	21	181	10.4	202	21	164	11.4	185
Fritz	313	124	71.6	437	310	122	71.7	432
Kiffer	71	171	29.3	242	71	156	31.3	227
Miller	72	136	34.6	208	71	124	36.4	195
North	10	154	6.1	164	10	140	6.7	150
Ridge	4	164	2.4	168	4	149	2.6	153
Moses	225	24	90.4	249	223	22	91.0	245
Valley	6	370	1.6	376	6	327	1.8	333
Williams	6	112	5.1	118	6	102	5.6	108
TOTALS	911	1473	38.2	2384	903	1340	40.2	2243

Table 6.13 contains the elementary pairings for the Clinton/Branch high school attendance area. The reassignments proposed in table 6.13 for the combined Clinton/Branch high school attendance area include the redistricting of the Miller and Kiffer elementary attendance areas, pairing the Fritz/Valley attendance area, and clustering the North/Ridge/Moses and the Anderson/Brown/Williams attendance areas.

TABLE 6.13. Assignments for the Elementary School Populations of the Clinton/Branch High School Attendance Area

School Pair	Proposed Grades	Capacity	Black	Nonblack	Black	Nonblack	% Black	Total
Miller	K, 1–6	540	169	310	169	310	35.3	479
Kiffer	K, 1–6	600	227	392	227	392	36.0	392
Fritz	K, 1–3	1,000	670	270				
Valley	K, 4–6	1,000	8	874	678	1,144	37.0	1,144
North	K, 1–4	510	42	360				
Ridge	K, 1–4	570	10	392	584	807	42.0	1,391
Moses	K, 5, 6	790	532	55				
Anderson	K, 5, 6	740	415	76				
Brown	K, 1–4	450	51	427	475	770	38.0	1,245
Williams	K, 1–4	400	9	267				

Table 6.14 shows the junior high school and table 6.15 the senior high school feeder patterns for the combined Clinton/Branch high school attendance area. In table 6.14, any junior high student living within the designated elementary attendance areas will attend the junior high school noted in the left-hand column. In table 6.15 any high school student living within the

TABLE 6.14. Junior High School Feeder Patterns for the Combined Clinton/ Branch High School Attendance Area

Junior High School Elementary Feeder Zone	Capacity	Approx. No. Jr. High Students		New Population			
		Black	Nonblack	Black	Nonblack	% Black	Total
Dunn	700						
North		10	154	239	342	41.1	581
Ridge		4	164	239	342	41.1	581
Moses		225	24				
Harwood	1,200						
Fritz		313	124				
Kiffer		71	171	390	665	36.9	1,055
Valley		6	370				
Griffith	1,000						
Anderson		125	37				
Brown		21	181	284	466	37.8	750
Miller		72	136				
Williams		6	112	118			

TABLE 6.15. High School Feeder Patterns for the Combined Clinton/Branch High School Attendance Area

High School Junior High Feeder Zone	Capacity	Approx. No. High School Students		New Populations			
		Black	Nonblack	Black	Nonblack	% Black	Total
Clinton							
Harwood		390	665	390	665	36.9	1,055
Branch							
Griffith		284	466				
				523	808	39.2	1,331
Dunn		239	342				

designated elementary attendance areas will attend the high school noted in the left-hand column.

Figures 6.9, 6.10, and 6.11 are mock-ups showing the configurations of elementary schools (6.9), the junior highs (6.10), and the contiguously paired Clinton/Branch high school district (6.11). School locations are shown in each figure by a star.

If the Clinton/Branch high school attendance area had been a noncontiguous high school pairing instead of a contiguous pairing, the same basic configurations would have been used. Figures 6.12, 6.13, and 6.14 show how these pairings would have been accomplished. It must be realized that in noncontiguous pairings additional transportation will be needed.

The following summarizes the feeder patterns established in the combined Clinton/Branch high school attendance district.

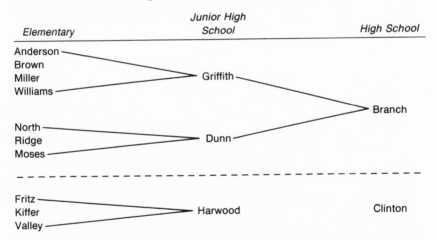

The development of a desegregation plan requires that the planner move in an orderly manner from redistricting to contiguous pairing to clustering to noncontiguous pairing. As stated, redistricting is the easiest and least disruptive way to desegregate a school community. Unfortunately, redistricting has a limited use; it is a rare plan that would not include several desegregative techniques.

FIGURE 6.9
Elementary Schools as Desegregated in the Branch/Clinton
High School Attendance District

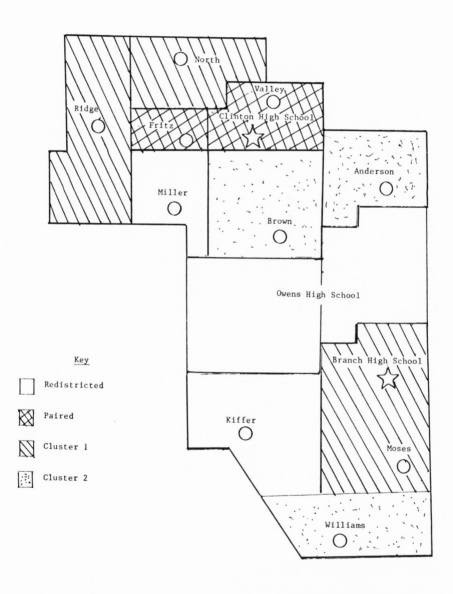

FIGURE 6.10
Junior High School Feeders in the Branch/Clinton
High School Attendance District

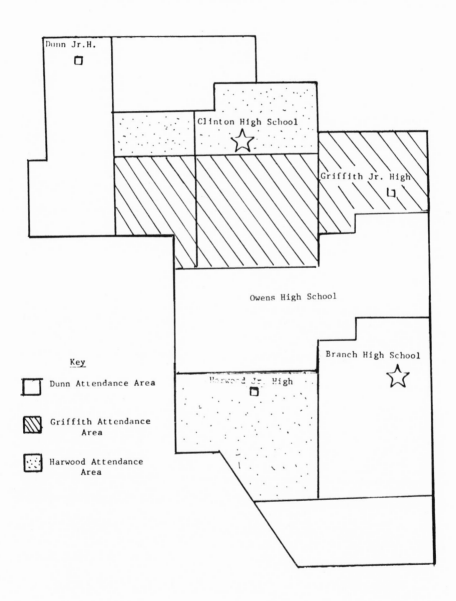

FIGURE 6.11
High School Feeders in the Branch/Clinton High School Attendance District

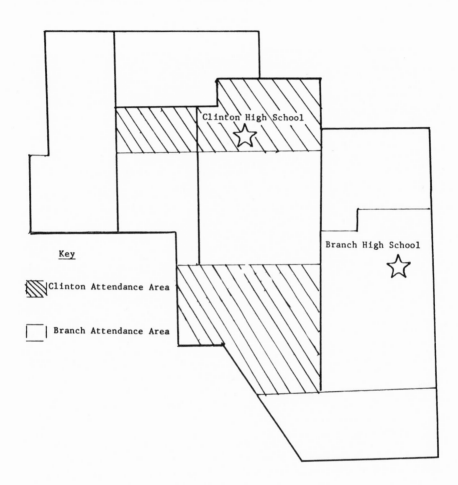

FIGURE 6.12
Elementary Schools as Desegregated in the Branch/Clinton
High School Attendance District

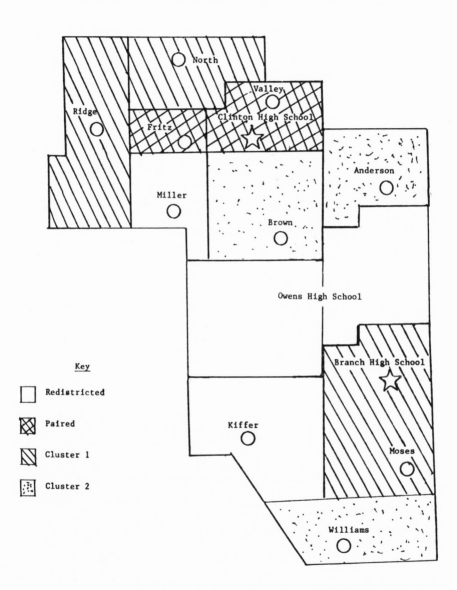

FIGURE 6.13
Junior High School Feeders in the Branch/Clinton
High School Attendance District

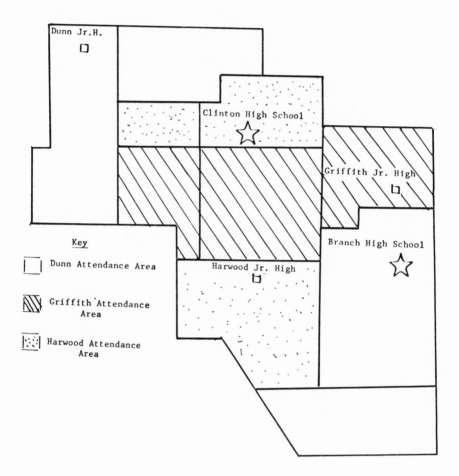

FIGURE 6.14
High School Feeders in the Branch/Clinton High School Attendance District

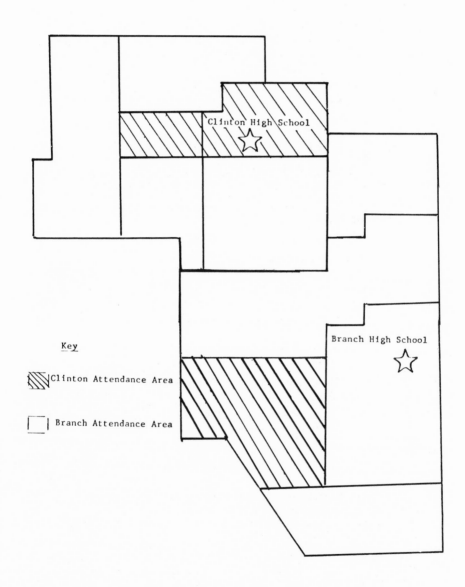

Key

Clinton Attendance Area

Branch Attendance Area

The figures and tables in this chapter illustrate how a hypothetical school system could be desegregated. These techniques will work in any school district—from systems with only one high school to systems with several hundred buildings. Of course, the more buildings, the more complicated the task, but the basic approaches remain the same. If students need to be transported, it must be kept in mind that distance between schools, though a factor, does not weigh as heavily in plan development as does the time it takes to get a student to a school.

Finally, the importance of accurate tables, consistent data, clear demographic information, and clearly stated parameters cannot be overemphasized. When a planner is inaccurate on any of these data, suspicion will be created about the quality of the entire plan. Plans become a matter of public record and must be able to withstand careful inquiry.

SELECTED COURT DECISIONS

Brinkman v. *Gilligan*, 503, F.2d 684, 704 (6th Cir, 1974); *Dayton Board of Education* v. *Brinkman,* 96 S.Ct. 433, 423 U.S. 1000, 46 L.Ed.2nd 376 (1977).

Green v. *County School Board of New Kent County, Virginia*, 88 S.Ct. 1689, 391 U.S. 430, 20 L.Ed.2d 716 (1968).

Higgins v. *Board of Education of Grand Rapids*, 508, F.2d 779, 787 (1974).

Winston-Salem/Forsyth County Board of Education v. *Scott* (N.C.), 92 S.Ct. 1236, 404 U.S. 1221, 31 L.Ed.2d 441 (1971).

SELECTED BIBLIOGRAPHY

Cronin, J. M. "City School Desegregation and the Creative Uses of Enrollment Decline." *Integrated Education* 15 (January 1977) 10–12.

Doughty, J. J., ed. "Desegregation Plans and Possibilities; Symposium." *Theory into Practice* 17 (February 1978): 1–90.

Legett, S. "Sixteen Questions to Ask, and Answer, Before You Close a Small School." *American School Board Journal* 165 (April 1978): 38–39.

NOTES

1. Care must be exercised here. It is true that handicaps occur without regard to race or ethnicity. Thus one would expect to find special schools to generally be racially nonidentifiable. When two or more schools for specifically handicapped children exist in a system, however they should not be racially identifiable.

2. Emptying some school buildings could provide facilities for some future magnet program or alternative educational opportunities for adults, students of special need, technical and vocational centers, and so forth.

3. In some instances, limits for pupil assignment are established by the court in the order for remedy. In most cases the court will provide some guidelines but will leave to the planner the flexibility to use his expertise and knowledge of the

school community. Even with these directions and flexibilities, it is wise to state in the beginning what the parameters for pupil assignment will be.

4. For example, a school system being desegregated has a systemwide ratio of 38 percent black and 62 percent nonblack. Using the factor of ± 15 percent, a school within the system is considered to be desegregated if its black population range is between 23 and 53 percent and its nonblack population is ranged between 47 and 77 percent.

5. If an elementary attendance area has a black/nonblack ratio of 70 percent black and 30 percent white, then the junior high school population and the high school population residing in the elementary attendance area will reflect within a few percentage points the black/nonblack ratio of the elementary population.

6. The courts have allowed a student freedom of choice if the transfer improves the racial balance of both the sending and receiving schools.

7. See chapter 5 for discussion of contiguous pairing.

7

Development of the Plan for Personnel Assignment

The placement of staff in a school system must avoid racial imbalance in the same way that the placement of students must. The difference between correcting racial imbalances on staff and among students is that staff reassignment is done individually and is less complicated to implement. Frequently, however, staff reassignments is every bit as conflict ridden. Recently, segregated patterns with respect to non-certificated personnel have also come under the court purview. Because important functional distinctions exist between administrative staff, teaching staff, and noncertificated staff, each is treated separately in this chapter.

Essential Conditions

As with the assignment of students, certain conditions must be established in order to judge whether a school district is racially balanced with respect to teaching personnel assignment and placement. The first essential condition is that the racial composition of faculty and staff in any school at any particular level (elementary, junior high, or senior high) shall, as nearly as possible, reflect the racial composition of all faculty and staff at the same level in the system as a whole. The only exception would be when the number of faculty at any given level was so disproportionate to the racial composition of the school system that simply reflecting the composition in any school building would still fall short of an acceptable racial ratio for the system. Therefore, instances occur when the only alternative to the racial balancing of a faculty and staff is to go into the open market and hire additional faculty for a given educational level. (Normal attrition and careful selection of replacements often obviate the need for this, however.) A teaching staff in a school is considered adequately composed racially if it reflects, within 5 percent, the racial composition of all teachers at that level within the system.[1]

The second essential condition that the plan must ensure is that faculty and staff with the greatest experience and training are evenly distributed throughout the system. With respect to experience and training, teachers can be placed into three categories: (1) those with zero to three years' experience, (2) those with four to seven years' experience, and (3) those with eight or more years.[2] When these categories are established throughout the system, with appropriate tolerances, an even distribution of teachers by level of experience will occur. This is based on the assumption that balancing on the basis of experience will be sufficient to assume a reasonable balance with respect to ability and training.[3]

Emphasis is placed on experience because many court guidelines, considering faculty assignments, require that no school have an inordinate number of beginning teachers or experienced teachers and that a reasonable balance be achieved with respect to degrees and training. Thus the commonly accepted practice of dividing faculty into "experience" categories has been established. Implied, of course, is that all assignments and reassignments will be made with appropriately certificated personnel.

TEACHING STAFF

Elementary and secondary schools are treated as two distinct groups. The elementary staff should balance within 5 percent of the minority/nonminority ratio within the school system. But the secondary staff usually is permitted to balance within 10 percent of the ratio within the system because the elementary school teacher is a generalist in education, whereas the secondary teacher frequently is a subject specialist. Therefore, it is less of a burden on the school system to balance elementary faculties more closely than secondary faculties.

Once the ratio of minority to nonminority staff is known, a by-school analysis must be made to identify schools that are outside the acceptable range for racial balance. After the schools are identified, a determination must be made of how many faculty need to be shifted in order to realize racial balance within each school. Table 7.1 shows the elementary faculty of one school system. Data have been presented in this format so that the planner can recognize immediately those schools that have racial imbalance.

One can see from the table that some school faculties within this system are out of racial balance. This means that the schools identified will have to make an adjustment in faculty assignment so that they no longer have racially identifiable faculties.

The same procedure is followed for secondary schools. The only difference is that, instead of a 5 percent tolerance, the tolerance used is 10 percent. As stated, the reason for the difference in acceptable variances is the specialization of secondary school staffs.

TABLE 7.1. Percentages of Minority and Nonminority Teachers Assigned to Elementary Schools

School	Teachers M^a	Teachers NM^a	Total Staff[b]	% M	% NM	Out of Balance[c]
Aaron Burr	16.47	7.60	19.07	60.14	39.85	X
A. G. Beal	9.00	27.40	36.40	24.72	75.27	X
Alfred	14.20	13.20	27.40	51.82	48.17	
A. J. Rickoff	18.10	9.66	27.76	65.20	34.79	X
Anthony Wayne	11.88	11.52	23.40	50.76	49.23	
Anton Dvorak	17.60	7.70	25.30	69.56	30.43	X
Barkwell	4.34	12.34	16.68	26.01	73.98	X
Beekins	16.00	7.40	23.40	68.37	31.62	X
Boulevard	13.50	10.80	24.30	55.55	44.44	
Buckeye	11.24	11.84	23.08	48.70	51.30	
Charles	14.90	10.04	24.94	59.74	40.25	X
C. W. Chesnutt	7.80	11.00	18.80	41.48	58.51	
C. T. Brewer	5.40	7.66	13.06	41.34	58.65	
Clanton	19.60	11.80	31.40	62.42	37.58	X
Watson	8.32	10.30	18.62	44.68	55.31	
Washington Irving	16.00	6.00	22.00	72.72	27.27	
Washington Park	1.86	4.94	6.80	27.35	72.64	X
Willow	7.40	5.24	12.64	58.54	41.45	X
Woodland Hills	13.20	14.58	27.78	47.51	51.48	
Woolridge	5.26	2.76	8.02	65.58	34.41	X
TOTALS	532.15	463.20	995.35	53.46	46.53	

SOURCE: School district personnel office.

[a]M = Minority; NM = nonminority.

[b]Fractions occur because some teachers are assigned to two or more buildings or have part-time administrative duties.

[c]A school is out of balance if it exceeds 48% minority or 52% majority with a 5% tolerance.

Reassignment of Faculty Personnel

In the reassignment of teachers to achieve racial balance, certain guidelines should be followed. First, the reassignments to schools should, wherever possible, be made within the approximate geographical area of the school where the teacher is currently teaching. This will not always be possible, but adhering to this policy is less disruptive for the individual because of the presumed location of residence and the usual driving pattern to and from work.

Second, every year new certificated staff are employed to fill vacancies created as a result of resignations, retirement, death, or new programs. Although it is impossible to predict the number of new staff that will be needed in any given year, an examination of historical data will provide some insight and permit reasonable estimates. The judicious placement of new staff members, on the basis of race and years of teaching experience, will provide a reasonable and systematic way to alleviate "out-of-balance" school facilities. This may not be totally sufficient to correct the existing situation because of an uneven attrition rate by school and school level. Care must be taken when adding new staff not to create a faculty with an inordinate number of beginners (0–3 years' experience) or career teachers (8 or more years' experience).

Third, when schools are recommended for closing, teachers in those schools will normally be reassigned. This reassignment should be made so that it promotes appropriate racial balances in the remaining schools. Here again, cognizance must be taken of years of teaching experience when reassigning so that faculties of individual schools reflect a reasonable balance of experience.

Fourth, a soliciting of volunteers for reassignment should be made. This list of volunteers will provide a pool for needed reassignments in schools that are out of racial balance.

If the above methods do not provide enough faculty to balance all the schools, lottery lists containing the names of all teachers except those who are on the volunteer list or who have otherwise been reassigned in a manner consistent with racial balance should be prepared. There should be six lists, based on race (nonminority and minority) and the three categories of teaching experience (0–3 years, 4–7 years, 8 or more years). When a specific category of teachers is needed to bring a school into balance, a lottery should be held from the appropriate list and a teacher assigned. Lottery lists for junior high, senior high, and vocational schools, and speciality teachers, have to be further categorized into certification areas·so that only appropriately certificated teachers are reassigned.

ADMINISTRATIVE STAFF

An examination of the racial makeup of the administrative staff must be made so that future recruitment and placement of persons to fill management and leadership roles in the system can be done on an equitable basis. Moreover, once data pertaining to current administrative assignments have been collected, some immediate attention to administrative reassignments can be made.

Building Administrators

Table 7.2 analyzes individual school building administrative teams of one school system being desegregated. The table reveals that of fifteen schools, seven seem to have administration teams that are out of balance. Some schools have a minority principal with three out of four assistants also minority, whereas other schools have nonminority principals and three of the four assistant principals nonminority.

In making judgments about whether building administrative teams are out of balance, the following guidelines are helpful:

1. Where there are two or three administrators, at least one of the three (but no more than two) should be a minority-group member.

2. On administrator teams of four or more, at least 25 percent of the team should be composed of either majority- or minority-group members. Where the number of the team is five or six, at least two should be majority- or minority-group members.[4]

We would recommend that reassignments be made so that all administrative teams within the school system have nonminority–minority administrative ratios of 60-40, with a deviation of ±20 considered reasonable.

TABLE 7.2. High School Building Administrative Teams, by Minority/ Nonminority and Position[a]

School	Principal		Asst. Principal		Out of Balance
	M^b	NM^b	M	NM	
Adams	1	0	2	3	
Booker T. Washington	1	0	2	1	
David T. Hughes	1	0	3	1	
Douglas	0	1	2	2	
Jackson	0	1	1	2	
Jane Addams	0	1	1	1	
Javits	0	1	4	1	
J. F. Kennedy	1	0	3	1	
John Hay	1	0	3	1	
Kevin	0	1	1	3	
Lincoln West	0	1	1	3	
M. L. King	0	1	1	1	
North Tech	0	1	1	0	
South Tech	0	1	1	3	
Wayne	0	1	1	3	
TOTALS	5	10	27	26	

[a]Frequently personnel occupying highly visible positions such as guidance counselors will be included in this analysis and reported as a part of the administrative team. A third column is then added, and these data are included in the analysis.

[b]*M* = Minority; *NM* = Nonminority.

Central Office Administrators

The school district committed to a desegregated setting needs also to examine staff assignments in the central office, and so an analysis similar to that conducted at the school building level must be accomplished. Often, because of past actions and current insensitivity (even in these days of affirmative action), a considerable imbalance will be revealed or certain positions within the administrative hierarchy will seem almost racially designated.[5]

Table 7.3 reveals the kinds of data needed to begin an analysis. All central office positions, line and staff, are examined according to the race of the incumbents. If the community evidences substantial diversity beyond the general categories of black and nonblack, it would be best to expand the

TABLE 7.3. Central Office Professional Staff, by Race and Position

Position	No. Black	No. Nonblack	Total	% Black	% Nonblack
Supt.	0	1	1	0	100.0
Asst. Supt.	1	3	4	25.0	75.0
Exec. Director	2	3	5	40.0	60.0
Director	2	27	29	6.9	93.1
Supv. I	1	3	4	25.0	75.0
Supv. II	4	36	40	10.0	90.0
Supv. III	2	9	11	18.2	81.8
Other	6	14	20	30.0	70.0
Nonadministrative					
Nonpublic	4	14	18	16.1	77.8
Nonadministrative					
Specialists, etc.	37	193	230	17.8	83.9
TOTALS	59	303	362	16.3	83.7

SOURCE: *Report of Professional Staff Assignment.*

nonblack category to include Native American, Chicano, Oriental, Puerto Rican, and so on.[6] Even a cursory review of table 7.3 reveals only a modest number of minority central office members, the large percentage of whom hold staff rather than line positions. This is suspect.

But the question often arises, can a district be expected to release competent administrators who may have provided excellent service to the district over the years in order to achieve desired desegregation? The answer to this is a qualified no. Often, normal attrition of central office staff because of retirements or resignations will be sufficient to create an opportunity for the system to develop diversity at the central office level. Again, care will have to be taken that this diversity is reflected at all levels and in line as well as staff positions.

In order to gain insights into possible upcoming vacancies, data such as that depicted in table 7.4 will be useful. One can see in the table that nine individuals in the central office have thirty or more years of experience and may be nearing retirement.[7] Recruitment of replacements in accordance

TABLE 7.4. Number of Administrators, by Years of Experience

Years of Experience[a]	Central Office	Elementary	Secondary	Total
32+	6	8	2	16
31	2	0	2	4
30	1	1	0	2
29	3	4	4	11
28	5	4	2	11
27	4	8	5	17
26	5	4	4	13
25	5	8	2	15
0–24	87	91	88	266
TOTALS	118	128	109	355

SOURCE: Division of Administration.

[a]Does not include military or industrial experience credit.

with affirmative action requirements might be sufficient to correct imbalances.

Recruitment and Reassignment of Administrators

Recruitment and reassignment of administrators to achieve balance might be harder to accomplish than with other professional personnel. Three factors can ease the transition. First, frequently as a result of desegregation, a number of schools are recommended for closing, but some schools reopen as alternative schools, requiring a number of reassignments. Candidates for reassignments to improve racial balance can come from this pool of displaced administrators. Moreover, as a result of schools closing and increased enrollment at other schools, additional administrators and guidance personnel are needed at the remaining schools. Care should be taken that these assignments are made with biraciality in mind. Second, some administrators are probably nearing retirement. Replacements for them should be made in a manner that ensures appropriate biraciality. Third, given the option, administrators frequently volunteer for new assignments, often seeking new challenges for themselves in a concern for professional renewal.

CLASSIFIED OR NONCERTIFICATED STAFF

One further analysis needs to be conducted before the issue of personnel assignment is resolved. More and more, courts and plaintiffs are raising questions about the racial and ethnic identifiability of certain noncertificated positions. Clearly, in many school systems certain positions are filled with a preponderance of one race or ethnic group. The degree to which this is true in any particular district must be examined, and if a district is racially imbalanced, appropriate steps should be taken to reduce the negative impact.[8]

Data such as those depicted in tables 7.5 and 7.6 are necessary. Table 7.5 shows a breakdown of classified employees by three typical school positions. Note the differences between "clerical" and "custodial." Is this pure chance? (The data, by the way, are real; the school names are not.) The courts and plaintiffs will think not. Table 7.6 shows data for a school system as a whole. Similar conclusions can be drawn for all levels of the system.

The desegregation of the professional staff of a school system requires an analysis of staff by categories and a systematic method of reassigning staff to realize racially balanced professional staffs throughout the school system. Students, minority and nonminority, should not see only one racial group dominating the teaching or administrative roles within a school system.

Similarly, a school system where all the nurses, secretaries, and aides are nonminority, and all the custodians and bus drivers are minority, depicts role models that are not acceptable. Care must be taken at every point in personnel assignments within the school system to see that the racial configuration of any personnel group is homogeneous enough to preclude racial identification with a role.

TABLE 7.5. Classified Personnel Employed in Elementary Schools, by Race and Position

Schools	Clerical B	Clerical NB	Custodial B	Custodial NB	Cafeteria B	Cafeteria NB	Total B	Total NB
Alger	0	1	3	0	0	1	3	2
Hill	1	0	1	1	0	0	2	1
Arlington	0	2	3	0	0	1	3	3
Bander	0	1	3	0	0	1	3	
Barton	1	0	1	1	0	0		
Basely Park	1	0	2	1	1			1
Beaumont Acres	0	1	2	1		1	0	4
Arkinson	0	1				0	4	1
Brammel			4	1	0	1	4	4
			0	3	0	1	0	6
	0	1	3	0	0	1	3	2
Creek	0	1	2	1	0	0	2	2
Wilson	1	0	4	0	0	0	5	0
Winters	0	1	2	1	0	1	2	3
Wonderland	0	1	2	1	0	1	2	3
Young	0	3	6	5	0	1	6	8
Zinn	0	1	1	2	0	1	1	4
TOTALS	13	132	264	97	28	84	305	313
%	9.0	91.0	73.1	26.9	25.0	85.0	49.4	50.6

SOURCE: Division of Research.

TABLE 7.6. Composites Classified Personnel in School Buildings, by Race and Position

Schools	Clerical B	Clerical NB	Custodial B	Custodial NB	Cafeteria B	Cafeteria NB	Total B	Total NB	
Elementary	13	129	257	90	28	82	298	301	
Junior High	16	51	142	28	35	131	193	210	
High Schools	11	78	130	57	26	95	167	230	
Spec. and Other	1	12	11	11	1	3	13	22	
TOTAL	41	270	540	186	90	311	671	763	1.434
%	13.2	86.8	74.4	25.6	22.4	77.6	46.8	53.2	

SOURCE: Division of Research.

SELECTED COURT DECISIONS

Augustus v. *Board of Public Instruction of Escambia County, Florida*, 306 F.2d 862 (1962). This case broke no new constitutional ground, but it did indicate that the courts would begin to examine the question of faculty desegregation.

Board of Public Instruction of Duvall County, Florida v. *Braxton*, 362 F.2d 616 (1964).

Carr v. *Montgomery County Board of Education*, 289 F.Supp. 645 (1968).

Johnson v. *San Francisco Unified School District*, 339 F.Supp. 1315 (1971).

Singleton et al. v. *Jackson Municipal Separate School District et al.*, 348 F.2d 729 (1965).

Penick v. *Columbus Board of Education*, 429 F.Supp. 229 (1977).

United States v. *Jefferson County Board of Education*, 380 F.2d 385 (1967).

United States v. *Montgomery County Board of Education* 395 U.S. 225, 89 S.Ct. 1670, 23 L.Ed.2d. 263 (1969).

SELECTED BIBLIOGRAPHY

Ayers, Q. W. "Racial Hiring Quotas for Teachers: Another Perspective." *Clearing House* 49 (November 1975): 105–7.

Berlowitz, M. J. "Institutional Racism and School Staffing in an Urban Area." *Journal of Negro Education* 43 (Winter 1974): 25–29.

Buxton, T. H. "Black and White Teachers and Desegregation." *Integrated Education* 12 (January 1974): 19–22.

Colquit, J. L. "Increase of Black Administrators in Metropolitan School Systems." *NASSP Bulletin* 59 (October 1975): 70–74.

Hudgins, H. C. *Public School Desegregation: Legal Issues and Judicial Decisions.* Topeka, Kansas: National Organization on Legal Problems of Education, 1973.

Love, Barbara J. "Desegregation in Your School: Behavior Patterns That Get in the Way." *Phi Delta Kappan* 59, no. 3 (November 1977): 168–70.

Scharffe, William G. "Staff Integration in the Saginaw Public Schools." *Phi Delta Kappan* 60, no. 9 (January 1979): 361–64.

NOTES

1. Frequently, a 10 percent deviation is permitted at junior and senior high schools because of special subject-matter certification required for teachers, which may limit reassignment options.

2. There is nothing inviolate about these experience divisions; they simply divide teachers into neophyte, intermediate, and career categories.

3. In the experience of the authors, this has shown itself to be a reasonable assumption.

4. The intent of the school district to promote multicultural and biracial administrative teams should be apparent. Absolute ratios are not normally the issue. An apparent sustained effort reflected in administrative teams composed partially of members of significant minority groups in the community in a proportion generally reflective of the makeup of the total population will be satisfactory for most inquiries. The issue is really the degree to which "affirmative action" is evident.

5. For instance, it is noteworthy that a preponderance of "staff development" officers and "human relations" specialists are black; a preponderance of "line" officers, white. A similar phenomenon can be observed when sexes are compared; females are less frequently found in line positions.

6. While this book focuses on desegregation, we would be remiss in this discussion of personnel assignments if we did not mention that good administrative practice would include attention to affirmative action with regard to sex as well.

7. It is getting more difficult to acquire good estimates of this, however. The effect that recent federal legislation removing provisions for automatic retirement at a certain age will have is as yet unknown. Some districts have reported that personnel are increasingly reluctant to indicate when they expect to retire.

8. This is often difficult to accomplish. Certain classified positions, if not "high status," are at least "steady jobs" for people and may be sought after, at least within "reasonable" expectations of a particular group, minority or otherwise. Desegregating these positions may cause widespread resentment. It may be perceived that at least one kind of regular employment is no longer certain. It may also result in people with the fewest employment opportunities being placed in an even less desirable position. It may visit the agony of desegregation on those least likely to be able to be philosophic about it. In other words, resentment may be high, depending on whose "ox is being gored" or, to continue the metaphor, "whose rice bowl is being emptied." Nevertheless, if one notices that nearly all the custodians are black or Hispanic, and nearly all the secretaries are Anglo-Saxon, it is time for something more than philosophic reflection.

8

Transportation

The transportation of children as part of the desegregation of a school system is an activity that generally receives the greatest criticism from the public. Many people will say, "I am not opposed to desegregation, I am opposed to busing." These people do not realize that it is usually not possible to have desegregation without vehicular transportation of some children.

Transporting children to schools is an old practice; children in rural areas have for decades had to travel to school in order to achieve a good education. The reorganization of schools in the 1950s and 60s, through merger and centralization of facilities, brought on even more pupil transportation. Many new school districts acquired enormous fleets of buses, and some children in sparsely populated areas were transported long distances for long periods of time. The length of time on the bus was justified because students received the benefit of a quality educational program. Few quarreled with this motive.

With the advent of court-ordered desegregation, there has been a new focus on school transportation. Not only have schools been found to be segregated but, in most cases, minority and majority populations live in segregated neighborhoods. Therefore, desegregation of schools has meant moving majority and minority children from the neighborhood school to another school, even if the distance was beyond reasonable walking—and in most cases it was.

Most of the early desegregation plans were drawn and enforced in the South. Those who developed these early plans remember studying several school districts after the plans were implemented and finding that no more children were being transported under the new plans than had been transported before the plans. In some situations the number transported was actually smaller because most black children in the district had been transported long distances to the few black schools in the system. Now, black and white children were transported so that they could be together; the previous system took them away from one another.

The issue was somewhat different as northern cities became involved in desegregation. Most northern urban school districts did not engage in extensive busing and thus did not have large bus fleets. Students in those systems who needed transportation either got to school on their own or used public transportation. Northern school districts that did engage in pupil transportation owned small bus fleets or contracted with private or public carriers for services as needed.

Desegregation brought a new set of transportation problems to the public schools of the North. They had to look at either the establishment of transportation systems or enlarging existing systems. This necessitated complex planning and the expenditure of large sums of money.

This chapter focuses on those activities necessary to develop an efficient transportation schema to implement a desegregation plan. The procedures discussed hold true irrespective of whether the plan is voluntary or court ordered.

DETERMINING THE NUMBER TO BE TRANSPORTED

After the children have been assigned to schools, the number of children to be transported must be estimated. There is a degree of subjectivity here. Whenever projections are made about the number of children to be transported in a desegregation plan, the planner should make generous, albeit well-thought-out, estimates. It is better to project the transportation of 20,000 and end up transporting only 15,000 than to project the transportation of 20,000 students and end up needing to transport 24,000.

The planner can utilize some shortcuts in estimating numbers of students to be transported. These methods consist of sampling the school system and then generalizing to the total school population. Though an experienced transportation planner can be very accurate with this type sampling, a more detailed study is recommended. The reason for a detailed approach is that the cost of the equipment and personnel is high, and any estimates that are too far from actual needs may be costly to the school system.

To determine the number of children to be transported, the following procedures are recommended:

1. The planner should look at the student assignment at each of the three instructional levels (elementary, junior high, and senior high) and determine how many students from each instructional level will be eligible for transportation. The final total will include all students.

2. The planner must then identify each school pair or cluster. The total population for each pair or cluster must be recorded. The planner will then total these school populations and multiply by a factor of 46 percent. This figure will give the planner the total number of students to be transported in each

instructional unit. Table 8.1 shows how a planner determines those students to be transported.

One can see from table 8.1 that if the school system has paired or clustered a total elementary population of 26,000, then approximately 11,960 of those students must be provided transportation to their new school assignment.

TABLE 8.1. Determination of the Number of Elementary Students to Be Transported

Pairs/Clusters	Projected Population
Pair A	
School M	600
School N	750
Pair B	
School X	550
School Y	680
Cluster C	
School Q	730
School R	820
School S	960
Pair N	
School D	460
School E	390
Total Elementary Children Assigned to a Pair or Cluster	26,000

Total × Transportation factor of 46% = Total transported
26,000 × 46% = 11,960

The same procedure is now repeated for junior high and high school students. The factor of 46 percent derives from the authors' experiences in plan development. Some contiguous pairings will not require any transportation because students can walk to their new assignments, just as they walked to their old assignments. Additionally, some parents will provide transportation to the students even if school transportation is available. Finally, high school students in many instances provide their own transportation. The factor of 46 percent has been shown to reflect adequately the number of students who will require transportation when a desegregation plan is implemented in an urban school setting. Nevertheless, if a planner has reason to believe that the factor of 46 percent is not realistic for a school system, a new factor must be developed. The one caution is to stay on the "high side" of the projection rather than the low side.

DETERMINING THE NUMBER OF VEHICLES NEEDED

Once the total number to be transported has been established, the number of vehicles needed can be determined. The information collected earlier is of prime importance. A hypothetical situation may help explain this:

Hypothetical District X (an urban school system)

Enrollment	80,615
Students to be transported (using 46% factor):	
elementary	17,334
junior high	10,155
senior high	9,587
TOTAL	37,076

The law in this state requires that all large vehicles be equipped to seat 65 passengers. The state reimbursement program is related to the 65-passenger vehicle. The average number of pupils transported per vehicle per day in this state is 118. Therefore, if 37,076 students need to be transported to District X, a total of 314 65-passenger vehicles are needed.

One must also consider the problem of vehicle disablement; additional vehicles must be added to accommodate this. Districts use different figures to determine the number of spare vehicles needed, but a figure of 10 percent has shown itself to be a good indicator. This allows a school district to have one tenth of its total fleet either in maintenance or long-term repair at any one time. Therefore, in District X, an additional 32 (31.4) vehicles are needed, which brings the total fleet to 346 vehicles.[1]

District X at present owns 222 vehicles to transport students. Of these, 93 vehicles cannot be put into general service because they are equipped to handle handicapped students. Moreover, 55 vehicles are used to transport nonpublic school students, as required by state statute. The remaining 74 vehicles have been used to transport children to special programs and to transport kindergarten students. Examination of the transportation schedule of these 74 vehicles indicates that it would be possible to use 25 of these vehicles for transportation related to desegregation. This 25 can thus be subtracted from the 346 needed, leaving 321 65-passenger vehicles to be secured.

Phasing

Whether the district is desegregating voluntarily or not, it may wish to "phase-in" total desegregation. Courts have seen fit to give permission for this because they realize the enormous cost and confusion involved in implementing complex plans.[2] Any phasing activity will have an impact on how many vehicles are needed at one time.

District X has decided to phase its desegregation activity. In year 1, it will desegregate staff; in year 2, the elementary schools will be desegregated; and by the beginning of year 3, all junior and senior high schools will be desegregated. This phasing requires the following schedule.

Phase 1. Year 1, September: no additional vehicles needed.

Phase 2. Year 2, September: a total of 162 additional vehicles needed. These vehicles should be delivered and ready for service by August.

Phase 3. Year 3, September: a total of 184 additional vehicles needed. These vehicles should be delivered and ready for service by August.

When all phases are implemented, a total of 346 65-passenger vehicles will be needed. Considering the vehicles owned and available in District X, a total of 321 vehicles must be ultimately purchased.

PURCHASING VEHICLES

The cost of the vehicles is directly related to the size of the unit and the options desired, as well as to those options necessary to meet state and local safety requirements. As noted, in District X all vehicles are to be 65-passenger and are to be equipped with automatic transmission, mobile page P.A., and two-way radios. Local school bus dealers have been asked to give an estimate of the cost on these units.[3] The price used for projection should be near the lowest bid. In District X the lowest bid was $19,160 per unit. This is the price for the model year in which phase 2 will be implemented. Phase 3 vehicle cost will be calculated to reflect a 6 percent increase in cost.

The time it will take for delivery of the vehicles from the date of the order must be examined. This is crucial if a court-ordered plan must be in effect at a specified time. In District X the minimum time was 180 days (6 months) and the maximum time 240 days. Because of the phasing plan, the time line was crucial. To ensure delivery, the vehicles for District X needed to be ordered no later than December of the year previous to the implementation of phases 2 and 3.

State departments of education frequently provide some reimbursement for the purchase of school buses, but these provisions vary throughout the nation. In District X the state would reimburse 35 percent of each unit, at a maximum price of $14,236 per unit. It would also pay for 35 percent of an $850 maximum for automatic transmission. The amount that could be reimbursed to District X, therefore, was $5280.10 per vehicle.

The following phase costs are projected for District X.

Phase 1. No additional transportation costs.

Phase 2. 137 vehicles will need to be purchased, delivered, and made ready for service by August. These vehicles will cost a total of $2,624,920. In addition, the 25 District X vehicles that do not have two-way radios will need to be equipped with same. These radios will cost an additional $21,100 ($844 per unit). The total cost will be $2,645,920. District X will pay $1,922,646 and the State $723,374. (state cost: $5280.10 × 137 vehicles = $723,374. District X cost: remaining cost of new vehicles plus $21,100 for 25 additional two-way radios = $1,922,646.)

Phase 3. 184 additional vehicles will need to be purchased by December of phase 2 and delivered ready for service by August of the next year. These vehicles will cost $20,310 per unit (6% cost increase reflected) for a total cost of $3,737,040. The cost for District X will be $2,765,501, and the cost for the state will be $971,539.

When phases 2 and 3 are implemented, the purchase of 321 vehicles and an additional 25 two-way radios for vehicles not equipped will be required. The total cost thus will be $6,382,960. The cost to District X will be $4,688,147, and the cost to the state will be $1,694,913.

NONRECURRING ITEMS

Several other transportation items, relating to maintenance, service, and storage of vehicles, also result in one-time costs. Much thought must be given to the location and security of maintenance and storage areas. These areas should be located near the point of vehicle utilization. In some instances the school district will have large storage and maintenance facilities; when this is so, the most economical process may be to enlarge those facilities.

Drivers of the new vehicles will have to be hired and trained. It is important to note here that human relations issues may surface in desegregation implementation, and bus drivers need to be prepared to handle those issues.

The use of adult monitors on buses is an optional consideration. Determining whether or not to have monitors is related to the potential for trouble during the early stages of desegregation. If necessary, monitors should be used for purposes of safety and for keeping order on the buses. When the potential for conflict subsides, monitors may be removed. If major problems arise, the school-community loss could be far greater than the initial investment for monitors. (In District X, monitors were used.)

The following additional nonrecurring items were found necessary in District X:

Phase 1. No additional expenditures for transportation required.

Phase 2. Establishment of three 60-vehicle compounds, a bus port, a 10,000-gallon gasoline storage tank with two pumps, and a telephone with two separate lines. These will cost $249,650 per compound. The total will be $748,950, exclusive of land (the land was owned by District X).

Establishment of a base radio unit in the 3 compounds and purchase of 10 hand held units for key school officials. Hand held units will cost $935 each for a total of $9350. Base systems will cost approximately $2000 each. Total for all units would be $15,350.

Establishment of an 8-bay centrally housed maintenance facility including one bay with automatic washing and cleaning equipment. This maintenance facility would cost $175,000 exclusive of land.

Training for 137 bus drivers and 137 monitors. This will cost an estimated $200 per person for a total of $54,800. (In this situation the state will reimburse District X at rate of $7 per trainee because State regulations permit a partial reimbursement on training costs.)District X's share is $52,882 and the States share is $1918.

Phase 3. Three additional 60-bus compounds, a bus port, a 10,000-gallon gasoline storage tank, and a telephone with two separate lines. This will cost $264,629 per compound. The total will be $793,887, exclusive of land (District X already owns). This price relfects a 6 percent annual inflation rate. There will be a saving of almost $45,000 if this third phase building is done concurrent with the second phase, thereby avoiding the inflation rate.

A base radio station in each of the three compounds and 10 additional hand-held units. Hand-held units will cost $992 each, for a total cost of $9920. Base stations will cost $2120 per unit. The total cost for all units will be $16,280.

Establish one 9-bay centrally housed maintenance facility including automatic washing and cleaning equipment. This facility will cost $185,500, exclusive of land.

Provide training for 184 bus drivers and 184 bus monitors. This will cost $212 per person, for a total of $78,016. The state will reimburse District X $7 per trainee. District X cost will be $75,440, and the state's share will be $2576.

Phases 2 and 3 will cost a total of $2,067,783. District X's share will be $2,063,289, and the remaining $4494 will be paid by the state. Table 8.2 depicts the one-time nonrecurring costs in summary.

TABLE 8.2. One-Time Nonrecurring Transportation Costs

Item	Phase 2	Phase 3	Total
Buses			
District X	$1,922,464	$2,765,501	$4,688,147
State	723,374	971,539	1,694,913
Total	$2,645,920	$3,737,040	$6,542,960
Bus compounds	$ 748,950	$ 793,887	$1,542,937
Radios			
Base stations	$ 6,000	$ 6,360	$ 12,360
Hand-held units	9,350	9,920	19,270
Total	$ 15,350	$ 16,280	$ 31,630
Maintenance and repair facilities	$ 175,000	$ 185,500	$ 360,500
Training			
District X	$ —	$ —	$ —
State	—	—	—
Total	$ 54,800	$ 78,016	$ 132,816
TOTALS	$3,640,120	$4,810,723	$8,450,843

OPERATIONAL COSTS

When a district plans for desegregation, it must anticipate a greatly expanded transportation system. This could result in a significant increase in operating costs. These costs are often overlooked or not well thought out by school officials. Hidden costs, or costs not planned for, can be embarrassing to school officials when they are revealed to the public and may result in a loss of public confidence. Moreover, the public has a right to know what any and all costs will be.

One important reason why these costs are overlooked is that schools have historically taken on new activities or programs and not adequately antici- pated the increased costs of these programs. Additionally, the transportation system in many school districts has been understaffed and operating below need for years. A large desegregation activity will not allow for merely add- ing to what is probably an already overloaded system. Thus, a comprehen- sive analysis of the entire transportation program is justified.

The major operational costs are for personnel. Salaries to drivers, mainte- nance personnel, mechanics, monitors, managers, and supervisors will reflect the largest part of the new costs. Vehicle maintenance, fuel, tires, insurance, and repair will account for most of the other costs. As mentioned earlier, it is important to have all the necessary personnel policies and salary schedules at hand when making calculations. For example, District X will have to plan as follows in order to implement the three phases. In phase 1, no additional expenditures are required. Phase 2 breaks down as follows:[4]

1. Seven qualified personnel for preventive maintenance, safety inspections, fueling, and start-up should be hired. The cost will be an average of $10,051 per person, for a total of $70,357.

2. Fourteen qualified personnel for major mechanical maintenance and repairs should be hired. The cost will be an average of $15,659 per person, for a total of $219,226.

3. Fourteen mechanics' helpers should be hired to assist mechanics in major maintenance and repairs. The cost will be an average $10,051 per person, for a total of $140,714.

4. One parts manager should be hired to keep inventory control and dispense parts and supplies. The cost will be $17,517.

5. One wash bay operator who will be responsibile for operation of the auto- matic cleaning equipment will be needed at a cost of $10,051.

6. One qualified gargage supervisor should be hired to manage, direct, and co- ordinate the vehicle maintenance and repair program. The cost will be $20,123.

7. Two miscellaneous laborers for garage cleanup and custodial work will be needed at a cost of $10,051 each, for a total of $20,102.

8. One hundred thirty-seven bus drivers should be hired at $12,620 each, for a total of $1,728,940.

9. One hundred thirty-seven monitors should be hired to aide and assist the bus driver for orientation and control of students transported by bus. The cost will be approximately $6000 each, for a total of $822,000.

10. Eight security guards to protect the three bus compounds and the one main- tenance facility will cost $11,340 each, for a total of $90,720.

11. One assistant bus supervisor should be hired to assist in general administra- tion and vehicle dispatching. The cost will be $20,123.

12. Cost of maintenance and repair, fuel, tires and tubes, and insurance for each

assigned bus will be $2066, for a total of $334,962. (The state will reimburse $83,741.)

13. The monthly telephone rate of three compounds and one maintenance facility will be $44.70 per month for each unit, for a total of $2146.

In phase 3, the following must be planned for:

1. Nine qualified personnel should be hired for preventive maintenance, safety inspections, fueling and start-up. The cost will be $11,533 per person for a total of $103,799.

2. Eighteen qualified personnel should be hired for major mechanical maintenance and repairs. The cost will be $16,142 per person for a total of $290,556.

3. Eighteen mechanics' helpers should be hired to assist mechanics in major maintenance and repairs. The cost will be $11,533 each for a total of $207,594.

4. One parts manager to keep inventory control and to dispense parts and supplies should be hired at a cost of $18,241.

5. One wash bay operator who will be responsible for operation of the automatic cleaning equipment should be hired at a cost of $11,533.

6. One qualified garage supervisor to direct and coordinate the vehicle and maintenance repair program should be hired at a cost of $20,847.

7. Two miscellaneous laborers should be hired for garage clean-up and custodial work. The cost will be $11,533 each for a total of $23,066.

In phases 2 and 3, operational costs will be $11,654,168. The state will reimburse District X $225,817 for the cost of maintenance, repair, fuel, tires and tubes, and insurance.

Table 8.3 summarizes the district's recurring operational costs in phases 2 and 3 (no costs are incurred in phase 1). Once the recurring cost items have been calculated, the transportation planning activity has been completed. The assignment of students to specific vehicles or routes will not come until just prior to the opening of the particular phase.

Time and Distance Factors

There is a need to indicate to the public the longest distance any one student will be on a bus. Distances and transportation time should be kept as low as possible. In District X the maximum number of miles any student had to travel was 11.5, and the longest period of time any student had to be on a bus was 46 minutes.

Transportation required to desegregate a school district is more than a public relations concern. It is true that "busing" students to desegregate schools often has resulted in emotional reactions by various segments of the public. In many instances the emotions were fed by poor estimates of costs or unrealistic expectations. It is incumbent on school desegregators to plan the transportation endeavor carefully, completely, and realistically.

TABLE 8.3. Recurring Transportation Costs (Operation)

Cost Categories		Phase 2	Phase 3	Total
Maintenance helpers	77–78	$ —	$ —	$ —
	78–79	70,357	80,731	151,088
	79–80	—	103,799	103,799
	Total	$ 70,357	$ 184,530	$ 254,887
Mechanics	77–78	$ —	$ —	$ —
	78–79	219,226	225,988	454,214
	79–80	—	290,556	290,556
	Total	$ 219,226	$ 516,544	$ 735,770
Mechanics helpers	77–78	$ —	$ —	$ —
	78–79	140,714	161,462	302,176
	79–80	—	207,594	207,594
	Total	$ 140,714	$ 369,056	$ 509,770
Parts manager	77–78	$ —	$ —	$ —
	78–79	17,517	18,241	35,758
	79–80	—	18,241	18,241
	Total	$ 17,517	$ 36,482	$ 53,999
Wash bay operator	77–78	$ —	$ —	$ —
	78–79	10,051	11,533	21,584
	79–80	—	11,533	11,533
	Total	$ 10,051	$ 23,066	$ 33,117
Garage supervisor	77–78	$ —	$ —	$ —
	78–79	20,123	20,847	40,970
	79–80	—	20,847	20,847
	Total	$ 20,123	$ 41,694	$ 61,817
Miscellaneous laborers	77–78	$ —	$ —	$ —
	78–79	20,102	23,066	43,168
	79–80	—	23,066	23,066
	Total	$ 20,102	$ 46,132	$ 66,234
Bus drivers	77–78	$ —	$ —	$ —
	78–79	1,728,940	1,798,125	3,527,065
	79–80	—	2,415,000	2,415,000
	Total	$1,728,940	$4,213,125	$ 5,942,065
Bus monitors	77–78	$ —	$ —	$ —
	78–79	822,000	871,320	1,693,320
	79–80	—	1,170,240	1,170,240
	Total	$ 822,000	$2,041,560	$ 2,863,560
Security guards	77–78	$ —	$ —	$ —
	78–79	90,720	97,096	187,816
	79–80	—	97,096	97,096
	Total	$ 90,720	$ 194,192	$ 284,912
Assistant bus supervisor	77–78	$ —	$ —	$ —
	78–79	20,123	20,847	40,970
	79–80	—	20,847	20,847
	Total	$ 20,123	$ 41,694	$ 61,817

TABLE 8.3. Recurring Transportation Costs (Operation) *(Cont'd)*

Cost Categories		Phase 2	Phase 3	Total
Maintenance repair,	77–78	$ —	$ —	$ —
fuel tires,	78–79	334,962	354,780	689,742
tubes and insurance	79–80	—	402,960	402,960
	Total	$ 251,221 [a]	568,305 [a]	819,526 [a]
Telephone cost	77–78	$ —	$ —	$ —
	78–79	2,146	2,274	4,420
	79–80	—	2,274	2,274
	Total	$ 2,146	$ 5,548	$ 7,694
TOTALS		$3,413,240	$8,281,928	$11,695,168

[a]Reflects a state reimbursement factor of 25%. Reimbursement in phase 2 will be $83,741 and in phase 3 $142,076. This is determined by mileage.

This chapter has contained a discussion of the important elements of an effective and efficient student transportation plan. We have attempted to illustrate the elements with realistic cost figures. There are two caveats, of course. First, dollar costs for items cited vary by community. Second, we live in an economy of rising costs, and this book is being written in 1979. An inflation estimate of at least 9 percent per year should be added to the costs.

SELECTED COURT DECISIONS

Swann v. *Charlotte-Mecklenburg Board of Education*, 91 S.Ct. 1267, 402 U.S. 1, 28 L.Ed.2d 554 (1971).

SELECTED BIBLIOGRAPHY

Busing for Desegregation. The Best of Eric, Number 15. Eugene, Ore.: Eric Clearing House on Educational Management, 1976. 5 pages (pamphlet).

Carrison, M. P. "Busing: Is That Really the Public's Complaint?" *Thrust* 8 (October 1978): 16–18.

Demont, Roger, ed. *Busing, Transportation and Desegregation.* Special Monograph No. 4, Management Series. Danville, Ill.: Interstate Printing and Publishers, 1973.

Flygare, Thomas. "Cross District Busing in the School Spotlight Again." *Phi Delta Kappan* 57, no. 6 (February 1976): 411–12.

Mann, J. S. "In Defense of Busing." *Educational Leadership* 34 (April 1977): 501–5.

Orfield, Gary. *Must We Bus? Segregated Schools and National Policy.* Washington, D.C.: Brookings Institution, 1978. 480 pages.

Ozman, Howard, and Sam Craver. "The School Busing Issue." In *Handbook on Contemporary Education*, edited by Steven Goodman. New York: Bowker, 1976.

Scherer, Jacqueline, and Edward J. Slawski. *The Social Context of Desegregation: Busing as Scapegoat.* Washington, D.C.: National Institute of Education, 1978. 25 pages.

Stuart, Paul T., and Frank Miskow. "ABC's of Running a Safe Transportation System." *American School Board Journal* 158 (November 1970): 40–44.

NOTES

1. The district might wish to schedule multiple routes for a particular bus and/or provide for different beginning and ending times for schools. Variations of starting times and the number of students a district is willing to place on each bus will greatly alter the number of vehicles needed.

2. The advantages of "phasing" when many new buses are required is obvious. Time is needed to order and take delivery of buses, normally six to eight months.

3. One should be careful to project costs only on the basis of the model year requested. Often the information is requested in one model year and the vehicles purchased in another model year. This makes cost projections inaccurate. A minimum of 9 percent per year should be added to cover unit-price increases.

4. All figures given for personnel wages are based on 1978 figures for the position in a midwestern city.

9

Educational Programming

Though the primary source of school desegregation is to achieve a racial mix, the desegregation planner must keep in mind that the primary mission of the school system is the education of students. This is a "soft" area in desegregation plan development. Courts have had a tendency to refrain from pronouncements pertaining to educational programming and in some instances have specifically acknowledged that their prime concern is an appropriate racial mix and that they cannot speak to the quality of the educational program.

But the issue usually raised in the media and by the public when a school system goes into a desegregation program is that of achieving "quality education." In some cases this concern for quality education is little more than a flim-flam by those who oppose desegregation. This is not to say that people concerned about quality education oppose desegregation, but a desegregation plan is designed to mix children of different races in an ongoing school setting. A school system that has a high-quality educational program prior to desegregation will have a high-quality educational program after desegregation. Conversely, a school system with a poor educational program prior to desegregation will have a poor educational program after desegregation. It must be conceded that in most communities unequal educational opportunities exist, and some children are not receiving the same quality of education that other children are receiving. This is sad but true. It is also correctable, although not by the act of desegregation.

THE ONGOING CURRICULUM

Positive Program Possibilities

With the desegregation of schools, educators are provided with an opportunity to make significant programmatic changes and present them as elements of the desegregation program. Levine and Havinghurst[1] recount the educational modifications implemented in Cincinnati, Houston, and Chicago. Basically, these urban school systems have seized on desegregation plans to establish magnet schools and alternative programs within the existing school structure. These magnet programs[2] also allow for the development of innovative educational approaches. New programs can greatly facilitate a desegregation effort, often because they are bolstered by the enthusiasm and optimism of their creators and have the intellectual freshness necessary for a healthy learning climate.

Other school systems have used school desegregation plans to implement totally new educational concepts, such as middle schools to replace the more traditional junior high schools. The introduction of a middle school allows opportunities for a clinical approach to instruction, continuous progress education, and an integration of the basic skills of the elementary grades with the discipline orientation of the secondary years.

With a new alignment of staff, as well as students, professional task forces can be impaneled to examine the existing curriculum and make recommendations for program alterations consistent with the needs of all learners. Activities of this nature allow individual staff members to jointly establish goals and objectives for the programs, as well as to share instructional methodologies. The products from task groups can be new curriculum guides, new instructional approaches such as team teaching and small-group instruction, new media materials that can be shared among the professional staff, new assessment materials and activities that focus on local needs, new learning stations and laboratory settings, or a variety of other instructional objectives and methodologies that did not exist prior to the desegregation. An unanticipated outcome often is a biracial faculty that works together effectively in any number of problem-resolution activities.

These positive programmatic spinoffs from a desegregation plan can, in effect, allow a school system to modernize its educational programs or alter its educational programs without the common resistance to change. At the same time, these new programs can provide a task-oriented way for a biracial staff to learn to work together.

Negative Program Possibilities

One commonly voiced concern is that a deterioration of education programs and individual progress will result from school desegregation. Though in theory this should not happen, in practice it is a real possibility. The cause for program deterioration occurs, in most cases, as a result of the attitudes and expectations of the professional staff and the administration.

When schools are desegregated, there is a tendency on the part of administrators to significantly alter the rules and procedures that govern the school. In some instances, stringent rules and regulations are developed, and the school becomes highly regulated. Generally these rules and regulations are enforced with severe punishments for transgressors and minimal reward for those who conform. Elaborate demerit systems and complicated due process procedures usually accompany the new policies. On the other hand, some school administrators, fearing or not understanding the needs of a portion of their student body, rewrite the rules and regulations so that they become vague and ambiguous, and thus unenforceable. When this occurs, the learning climate becomes chaotic because teachers and students have no yardstick for acceptable behavior or consistent procedures. Chapter 11 describes in more detail what can happen when extremes are the case. Suffice it to say here that neither despotic rule nor laissez-faire hopefulness is adequate. Even worse may be a vacillation between the two.

Schools that allow their operations to gravitate toward either extreme will do violence to the educational programs being conducted. Students do not learn efficiently in schools that are run like concentration camps; neither do they learn in school systems that are in constant chaos. There must be mechanisms within the schools to maintain order, but these mechanisms must also facilitate learning. One group of students, because of race, economic circumstance, or newness in the building, should not be treated in such a way that they never become a part of the new educational institution.

The professional staff must also maintain constant standards of performance for all students, even though a change in racial composition has occurred. Ability grouping and tracking are probably the most extreme manifestations of teacher attitudes and expectations. Many schools develop plans for ability grouping and then implement those plans in a way that resegregates the student body. This resegregation of students, through labeling, has adverse effects on learners' self-concepts and reinforces prejudicial attitudes toward racial groups.

Attitudinal factors greatly influence the quality of educational program and the behavior and attitudes of the students who participate in the schools. These factors must be addressed through intensive staff inservice programs and staff renewal.

NONCOPING YOUTH

Policies to maintain positive control of students are important to the educational programs in any school, but especially in a school that has recently been desegregated. There are significant numbers of noncoping youth in every school in this nation; these students, regardless of race, place special educational demands on school programs. The problems caused by these youth are often exacerbated when they are reassigned to a new educational setting as part of a desegregation program. Frequently the implementation of a desegregation plan seems to cause disruptive behavior. Some students flaunt rules, accost classmates and teachers, become truants or become violent in school. Some of this is a natural consequence of a circumstance that increases individual anxiety; some is just a natural consequence of interacting adolescents. In any case, such behavior must be dealt with quickly, fairly, and sensitively by administrators and teachers.[3]

Frequently, however, there is a need for programs designed to accommodate noncoping students. Programs such as tutorial programs, laboratory or action-based programs, personal and vocational counseling, and small-group or individual instruction tends to have a positive effect on noncoping students.[4]

A ready accommodation must be made for noncoping youth in a newly desegregated school because this group of students may cause great disruption in the educational setting and do harm to the total learning environment of the school. Once a school begins to gain a reputation for disorder, violence, high truancy, and racial unrest, the professional staff loses control of the educational program and a general eroding of the quality of instructional offerings ensues. When this occurs, a general dissatisfaction can be noted in the community.

FEDERAL SUPPORT

Emergency School Assistance Act

As a result of desegregation activities that have taken place in the past ten years, the federal government has begun to address the programmatical aspects of school desegregation. One of the most direct ways that the government has become involved in educational programs is through the Emergency School Assistance Act. (ESAA). This act came into being in 1974 and since that time has provided funds for school systems engaged in desegregation. Funds are secured on a competitive basis and can be used only to remedy problems created by desegregating the school system. That is, funds cannot be used to implement a desegregation plan; they can be used only to remedy problems occurring after the plan has been implemented.

Generally, ESAA funds have been used to develop human relations programs for students, parents, and professional staffs. Human relations programs are designed to establish understandings between the affected groups and facilitate the positive participation of the groups in the educational setting.

A second important programmatic area where ESAA funds are used is in the provision of remedial programs in the basic skills. Many youngsters who come from racially isolated schools have deficiencies in their basic skills. Thus these students arrive at their new school at a developmental disadvantage because of their previous segregated instructional setting.

Another area for ESAA fund support is in the development of magnet schools. This relatively new dimension of ESAA funding is a direct involvement of the federal government in program remedies to school segregation. Special ESAA funds have been made available to a number of urban school systems, and a variety of innovative magnet programs have been established. Unfortunately, these magnet programs tend not to have a wide appeal and also to attract more minority than majority students. Majority students, especially those from middle- and upper-class backgrounds, tend not to participate in magnet programs, even though the programs are highly innovative in their focus. Majority middle- and upper-class students tend not to choose any program that requires entry into a learning setting that deviates from the traditional college preparatory model.

Such judgments could be premature. ESAA funding for magnet programs is new, and expenditures to date have been modest. Nevertheless, there are indications that these programs are not receiving wide support and that the programs themselves lack the vitality and originality to attract large groups of students.

Many other programs can be, and are, supported by ESAA funds. The two mentioned here are the most common areas for this support. The desegregation planner must keep in mind, however, that these funds are *not* available to school systems for the purpose of implementing a school desegregation plan. Thus, for example, if a desegregation plan called for special programs in remedial instruction, the school system would not be eligible for ESAA funds to pay for the program. But if, as a result of the desegregation, a need for remedial instruction arose, the school would be eligible for ESAA funding at that time.

This seeming "Catch-22" can be very important to the school system being desegregated. Though it appears to be a mere technicality in the law, it can have a real effect on programs and on eligibility for funds. A desegregation plan that is very specific in its program recommendations can cost a school system several million dollars in federal fund eligibility. Even where "quality edication" has become a rallying point in the community, the desegregation planner must resist the temptation to write specific program recommendations into the plan.

Federal "Title" Programs

Programs such as Title I of the Elementary and Secondary Education Act (ESEA) have caused the greatest concern for school administrators engaged in desegregation plan development. In many instances, the desegregation of a school system will alter not only the racial but the economic composition of a school. When this occurs, a school could lose its Title I funds because of a drop in the percentage of its disadvantaged population. Though a particular building might lose its eligibility for some funding, this does not mean that the school system will lose the funding it previously received, because the system will have approximately the same percentage of disadvantaged students after desegregation that it had before desegregation.

With the involvement of a great number of school systems in court-ordered desegregation, laws that restrict the use of monies for disadvantaged students will in all probability come under some redefinition. Though these laws are beyond the purview of this book, and are outside the jurisdiction of the courts, they are subject to influences from public school administrators and congressmen. The general rule that the courts have followed is that if a school system has a choice between losing its federal funding and desegregating the school system, the federal funding will be the item of lesser importance.

Another source of federal financial involvement is through community-action programs of the Justice Department and Title IV programs of the Elementary and Secondary Education Act. These two programs provide limited support to school systems as they enter into desegregation. Guidelines for assistance under these programs vary from year to year, and the amount of funds available is much less than under ESAA. Technical assistance to the school system through the offices that administer the program is generally forthcoming after a survey of needs and after a program design for a specific population is developed.

SPECIAL FEATURE PROGRAMS

Many school systems have special feature programs. These programs, if they serve a unique population, and if the population is composed without racial consideration, will usually be allowed to continue even when they do not fit the desegregation guidelines. Programs that serve the blind, deaf and severely physically or mentally handicapped all fall into the special feature program category. Care must be taken, however, because with the implementation of P.L. 94–142, many students who formerly were specially housed now must be "mainstreamed" into regular classrooms. Students who come under the requirements of P.L. 94–142 would be expected to participate on an equal basis in a desegregation plan.

Other special feature programs that may not be included in a desegregation plan are programs offered in a community school setting, programs offered to unwed mothers, or programs offered to the very old or very young. These programs, because they focus on unique and in most instances voluntary populations, will usually be allowed to continue in their existing state and not be made part of a desegregation plan.

KINDERGARTEN AND EARLY CHILDHOOD PROGRAMS

Kindergarten and early childhood programs usually do not become part of a desegregation plan because, in most instances, these programs are only part-time and are voluntary. Because of these two features, the courts have reasoned that to desegregate these programs would provide an unnecessary hardship on children and would have little impact on the desegregation of a school system. In most instances, a simple statement by the desegregation planner to the effect that kindergarten and early childhood programs will not be included in the plan will be sufficient for the court.

BILINGUAL PROGRAMS

With large populations of Hispanic students, plus pockets of Vietnamese students who have been displaced into our society, we have seen the rise of federal- and state-supported bilingual programs. These programs, because they serve unique populations, are generally given special consideration when desegregating a school system. In most instances courts will direct a desegregation planner to desegregate the school system but keep the bilingual programs intact. Thus, if a group of Hispanic students is reassigned for desegregation reasons, then the bilingual programs that existed in their former schools must also be provided in their newly assigned schools. This simply means that the planner must be careful to make provision for students who need bilingual programs.

CO-CURRICULAR PROGRAMS

Co-curricular programs can cause a desegregation planner great concern, because an important portion of the school program, especially at the secondary level, includes co-curricular activities. These activities include clubs, student governments, school publications, music and drama organizations, and interscholastic and intramural athletic programs. Therefore, when planning for the desegregation of a school system accommodations must be made so that any student who desires to participate in a co-curricular program may do so.

The courts have also held that the schools are responsible for transporting students who participate in co-curricular programs when their participation requires them to stay beyond the regular school day. This means that additional transportation requirements must be budgeted into the transportation portion of the plan.

Co-curricular activities are important to school desegregation because they allow students to mix in an informal setting. This mixing facilitates socialization and thereby the understandings sought by school desegregation. Sponsors, advisers, and coaches of these programs must realize this added importance of the activities. Activities should be designed so that they are an extension of the school curriculum, have wide participation, and fulfill educational needs.

Regardless of how a school system is desegregated, the school's primary mission is still realized through the educational programming. This means that though a plan for racial mixing has been decided on, the focus must still be on accommodating each student in a learning setting that fits educational needs.

If academic integrity is to be maintained, the programs must not be influenced by predetermined attitudes about the learning abilities of racial groups. The school program must be designed to accommodate the needs of all students.

Some influences on the learning climate are under the direct control of the teaching and administrative staffs of the school. Schools that allow resegregation through ability grouping or through sanctioned racially oriented activities will not realize the quality education desired. Additionally, schools with inconsistent discipline policies or with discipline policies that are either extremely harsh or condescending will interject chaos in the learning setting that will be detrimental to the overall program.

The most significant aspect of programming and desegregation is that the desegregation plan may provide the impetus for a school system to modify existing programs and upgrade programs that are no longer serving student needs. These opportunities for school systems to rearrange their learning climates can be fleeting, and a school system is well advised to take advantage of each opportunity.

Finally, the programs that frequently come under scrutiny are co-curricular activities that are both educational and social in nature. These programs have high visibility and are programs in which students have the greatest informal interaction with one another. They are programs that can have much positive effect on the desegregation plan. If co-curricular programs are arranged so that only one racial group participates, this will have a negative effect on the overall educational climate.

SELECTED COURT DECISIONS

Hobson v. *Hansen,* 269 F.Supp. 401 D.D.C. (1967).

Morgan v. *Kerrigan* (Mass.) 379, F.Supp. 410 (1974).

Pasadena City Board of Education v. *Nancy Anne Spangler,* 44 U.S.L.W. 5114 (1976).

Taylor v. *Board of Education of City School District of City of New Rochelle,* 195 F.Supp. 231 (1961).

SELECTED BIBLIOGRAPHY

Bash, James H. *Effective Teaching in the Desegregated School.* Fastback 22. Bloomington, Ind.: Phi Delta Kappa Educational Foundation, 1973. 46 pages (pamphlet).

Bernhard, G. "Desegregation Works." *National Elementary Principal* 56 (November 1976): 69–70.

Berry, Ray. "Integration Update." Riverside Unified School District, California, April 1978. 15 pages. Mimeographed.

Brookover, Wilbur; Charles Berry; Patricia Flood; John Schweitzer; and Joe Wisenbaker. *Schools Can Make A Difference.* Washington, D.C.: National Institute of Education, 1977. (NIE–G–74–0020)

Crain, Robert, and Rita Mahard. *Desegregation and Black Achievement.* Durham, N.C.: Institute of Policy Sciences and Public Affairs, 1977.

Edelman, Marian Wright. "Twenty Years After 'Brown': Where Are We Now?" *New York University Education Quarterly* 4 (Summer 1974): 2–10.

Fellman, David, ed. *The Supreme Court and Education.* Third ed. Classics in Education #4. New York: Teachers College Press, Columbia University, 1976. 326 pages.

Gordon, Edmund W. *A Comparative Study of Quality Integrated Education.* New York: Institute for Urban and Minority Education, Teachers College, Columbia University, 1976.

Havinghurst, Robert J. "Providing for Disaffected Youth." *Educational Leadership.* 34, no. 6 (March 1977).

Hughes, Larry W., and Gerald C. Ubben. *The Secondary School Principal's Handbook: Guide to Executive Action.* Boston: Allyn and Bacon, 1980.

Levine, Daniel U. *Models for Integrated Education.* Worthington, Ohio: Charles A. Jones, 1971. 115 pages.

Metz. Mary Haywood. *Classrooms and Corridors.* Berkeley: University of California Press, 1978.

Pettigrew, T. F. *A Study of School Integration.* Cooperative Research Project No. 6-1774. Cambridge, Mass.: Harvard University Press, 1970.

Sanders, Stanley G., and Janice S. Yarborough. "Achieving a Learning Environment with ORDER." *Clearing House* 50, no. 3 (November 1976): 100–102.

NOTES

1. Daniel U. Levine and Robert J. Havinghurst, *The Future of Big City Schools* (Berkeley, Calif.: McCutchan, 1977).

2. A more complete description of magnet programs is provided in chapter 2.

3. A good discussion of maintaining positive control of students can be found in Larry W. Hughes and Gerald C. Ubben, *The Secondary School Principal's Handbook: A Guide to Executive Action* (Boston: Allyn and Bacon, 1980).

4. See Stanley G. Sanders and Janice S. Yarborough, "Achieving a Learning Environment with ORDER." *Clearing House* 50, no. 3 (November 1976): 100–102.

10

Implementing a Plan

After a board of education approves a desegregation plan or a court mandates a plan, a number of important factors can affect the successful implementation of the plan. Overlooking these factors can seriously reduce the effectiveness of even the most carefully drawn plan. These factors relate, for the most part, to human behavior and the difficulties individuals and groups have in adjusting to change. Experiences in other situations allow us to forecast the difficulties and plan to deal with and overcome them.

The court should be extremely careful in drawing its final order to the school district. If the order is drawn improperly, it could cost the district large amounts of money that could otherwise have been saved. The order should also speak to some way of monitoring the plan mandated in the order. If the monitoring activity is not drawn tightly and is not put in the hands of responsible citizens, the court will find itself continuously involved in the management of a school district.

If the court order is well drawn and there is limited confusion in the application, the scope of the people problems that always accompany changes of great social significance are reduced. These problems relate to positions taken by local leaders in their criticism or support of the order and plan to be implemented. The position taken by leaders affects other citizens in the community and students who must attend the schools. The turmoil created through the efforts of parents and students who believe they are doing what the majority want can disrupt the implementation progress. Local governmental agencies that have jurisdiction when such disruption takes place must act swiftly, but with compassion, to avoid violence.

School officials must proceed in a positive manner to carry out a court order, understanding that the place for disagreement is in and through the legal process. Many administrators and teachers have never taught a multiracial group and do not know how to behave when working with people from orientations different from their own. The biases held by some ethnic groups about others must be dealt with, and their impact on the desegregated situation reduced.

The school must reach out to deal with different student and parent groups. The administrator-parent and teacher-parent relations must be improved through intensive interaction. Permanent councils or action groups that have dealt with the issues must be involved in positive ways to deal with problems that may arise and assist in predicting problems and helping school officials to overcome them. The school needs to make sure that facts are released and rumors controlled.

Even though the courts have directed public schools to desegregate, the effective implementation of a desegregation plan is not the sole province of the school. Many communities have not accepted this responsibility, and the schools and the community have suffered. One can observe many situations in which citizens have refused to pass tax levies for schools because of their disagreement with desegregation and their placing of blame on the schools. This form of protest can have serious long-range effects not only on the implementation of a plan but on the ability of a school system to provide quality education.

COMMUNITY MONITORING AGENCIES

Prior to the drawing of the court order, the school district should consult with the judge, either through the superintendent or through a lawyer. Often the court will appoint a master in the remedy or planning stage, and the master can assist the court and the schools. The court order should include, along with the expected legal definitions, the appointment of a desegregation monitoring committee. The order should designate the names of members and the organizations they will represent. It should also define exactly what the committee will be expected to do. Some examples of what these committees do follow:

Detroit, Michigan. In August 1975 Judge Robert E. DeMascio stated that monitoring was "an essential part of a sincere desegregative effort." The court appointed a monitoring commission to oversee and report to the district court judge on the progress of the Detroit desegregation plan.

The judge specified the creation of 12 subcommittees, most of which related to the educational components of the school district. The monitoring group then had to develop a design for a monitoring system; recruit, train, and assign monitors to schools; develop criteria to evaluate implementation of desegregation activities; and receive/review information from community groups at regional level and junior high school areas.

Boston, Massachusetts. In the fall of 1974, amid continuing litigation, the Boston public schools opened under Phase I of a desegregation plan. Serious public disorders hindered implementation throughout that school year. On June 5, 1975, Federal District Judge Garrity endorsed plans of the four court-appointed masters regarding citizen participation.

Basically, the judge expected a Citizens Coordinating Commission (CCC) to foster public awareness and involvement in the process of implementation of the court's desegregation orders. It was to be the primary body monitoring implementation on behalf of the court, and it was to assist the court, the school committee (board of education), school personnel, students, parents, and others to recognize and resolve problems faced in desegregation. The group was also to study the short- and long-term effects of school desegregation. One of the CCC's earliest tasks was to set up a monitoring system to audit the progress of desegregation activities.

In the school system, the CCC was given the task, too, of planning and overseeing the establishment of community councils.

Dayton, Ohio. On February 11, 1975, the court appointed the Dayton Citizens Advisory Board. Its charge was to (1) coordinate the efforts of all community agencies and interested persons in implementing the court's desegregation plan; (2) provide community education as to the requirements of the desegregation plan regarding transportation, services, and facilities; (3) receive comments, criticisms, and suggestions of people in the community regarding execution of the plan; (4) assist the community in working out problems with the school administration and report to the court as to the nature and resolution of such problems; (5) provide a system of monitoring the desegregation plan on a continuing basis and suggest changes when they appear to be advisable; (6) report periodically to the court and to the parties involved on the execution and implementation of the plan; and (7) provide other services as the court assigns them.

Denver, Colorado. The Denver Community Education Council (CEC) was appointed by U.S. District Court Judge Doyle on April 30, 1974, requiring desegregation of the Denver Public Schools. The citizen council was to serve as a monitoring committee charged with (1) coordinating implementation of the court desegregation plan and educating the community as to the court's findings; (2) educating the community as to the provisions and services of the school system; (3) receiving and considering comment, criticism, and suggestions and assisting in working them out and reporting the results to the court; and (4) generally monitoring progress and reporting to the court.[1]

The success of the monitoring committee depends on (1) the manner in which the presiding judge initiates and attends to matters assigned to the citizen group; (2) how the citizen group assumes its responsibility, the clarity with which it understands its mission, and the manner in which it expands its capabilities; (3) the attitudes and degree of cooperation from school officials and school employees; and (4) the responses of the community to the monitoring commission.[2]

The court order should also be carefully worded so that the court will allow the school district to get maximum financial support from other responsible institutions. The court should designate that the state is also responsible for supplying part of the costs for remedy. During the time in which the school was participating in segregative activities, the state supplied some financial support. It is therefore only logical that the state should participate in the remedy.[3] Without a court order, it will be more difficult for the school district to get the state support it needs.

The other source for financial support is the federal government. In 1974 Congress passed the Emergency School Assistance Act, which makes money available to school districts involved in desegregating their schools. The ESAA pays for certain activities not mentioned in the court order but which accrue to a school district because of the order. The ESAA will pay for inservice training for teachers and administrators so that they might be better prepared to take an active part in the implementation of the desegregation plan. It is important to emphasize that the federal government will not pay for the implementation of a plan, but will provide money to help remedy certain problems caused by implementation.

POLITICAL AND GOVERNMENTAL LEADERS

When desegregation litigation and subsequent planning for a remedy is in process, the public statements made by political and governmental leaders assume great importance. If they make negative comments, these will have a tendency to incite the public. In 1976, the U.S. Civil Rights Commission conducted studies of several desegregation plans then in operation.[4] They found that statements made by local political leaders were of great consequence in cities where there had been violence and turmoil. They specifically referred to Boston and Louisville, where local leaders did not speak and act positively about desegregation. Many political leaders are concerned about standing up for desegregation because of perceived political consequences. A cursory look at the history in these situations would tend to indicate that strong stands against the implementation of federal court orders to desegregate schools have not been particularly helpful to those politicians who have taken them. A particular case in point would be the stance taken by the governor of Florida in the Manatee County desegregation activity. He stood firmly against desegregation, which was thought to be a popular position, but he was defeated in the next gubernatorial election.

There are no sure ways to determine what position a local political leader might take. Nevertheless, providing information to leaders during the different stages of desegregation is recommended as a way toward more successful implementation. There should be no big surprises given to leaders about what is going to happen. It is also important to have several leaders appointed to the monitoring committee.

INVOLVEMENT OF THE COMMUNITY

The community is crucial to the successful implementation of any school desegregation plan. An aroused citizenry or a community that has been deeply divided over the issue of desegregation must be calmed in order to implement a plan properly. Parents of children involved in a desegregation plan must understand that their child's educational program will not be diminished in quality, nor will the child be put in physical danger.

In order to allay community fears and inform the community about the components of the desegregation plan, a substantial educational and informational program should be undertaken by the school system. This program should include neighborhood meetings, professional and business group meetings, and meetings with school-related organizations. These meetings will form the basis for informing citizens about the plan and allowing citizens to ask questions and express concerns.

In addition to meetings, there should be extensive explanations in local newspapers and on local radio and TV stations. These reports to the public should be frequent and should provide the latest information about what is happening in the desegregation activity. The most difficult period is the time between the issuance of the court order and the actual assignment of students to specific schools. A large amount of misinformation is usually available then. School officials should move as quickly as possible to assign students to schools and hold meetings with parents of the newly desegregated schools. These meetings can do a lot to reduce the anxiety of parents and should take place before the opening of schools.

Once the plan has been implemented, it is wise to have a series of planned experiences for parents within the newly desegregated schools. These experiences can include open houses or special evening programs. Opportunities should also be created for parents to assist in school programs on a voluntary basis and for parents to assist in the monitoring of the transportation components.

The federal government, through ESAA funding, makes money available for inservice training for parents. Inservice training experiences can range from simple talk groups to instructing parents in the techniques of teaching or tutoring in basic skills like reading and mathematics.

The community must be aware that the school intends to deal with problems as they arise. A hotline where parents can inform the school about what is going on and also get information has been a successful technique. A hotline can serve as a rumor-control center and allow parents to have information with which to combat the rumor mills. Hotline locations should be staffed with parents and professional school personnel. Care must be taken to ensure that all information is accurate.

Finally, a newsletter is helpful in informing the community. Parents are anxious to know about school activities and problems on a formal basis. A newsletter is already part of many school systems' public relations activities; only the focus need be changed during the early stages of desegregation.

Effective community involvement techniques and information dissemination devices are crucial to the initial success of the desegregation plan. The following quote may put the issue in perspective:

There does exist a leadership structure on the neighborhood level. This is especially important to the school system because the individual school building is the public welfare delivery system that is closest to the people—geographically as well as psychologically. Individual schools, thus may serve as most effective mechanisms to receive information from and dispense information to neighborhood power groups. There is much research to suggest that most individual decisions to support or not support a community issue are based on the influence of friends and neighbors rather than on outside data. Thus, it would be the astute educator indeed who becomes familiar with and has good communication with the leadership structure of the neighborhood.[5]

STAFF INSERVICE TRAINING

Though the programs offered in newly desegregated schools may remain basically the same, staff problems will crop up that relate directly to the change to a desegregated system. Administrators and teachers find themselves in a new and different environment. Many teachers have not taught in a classroom where students come from different ethnic and cultural backgrounds. Administrators find themselves dealing with different discipline problems. Several problems have been found in other desegregated situations:

1. Teachers and administrators hold low expectations for academic performance of minority children.

2. Teachers and administrators do not recognize that the typical instructional materials they use do not include minority viewpoints.

3. Teachers and administrators do not realize that treating students differently as it relates to race creates poor interpersonal relationships.

4. Teachers and administrators fail to recognize the contributions of minority children.

5. Teachers and administrators often group children for instruction based on factors unrelated to their abilities.

6. Teachers, administrators, and guidance counselors show bias in their counseling practices.

7. Administrators allow biased institutional practices to continue because of tradition.

8. Teachers and administrators fail to relate to minority students as individuals.

9. Teachers and administrators show bias in their administration of discipline.

10. Teachers and administrators do not exhibit honesty in dealing with issues.[6]

These problems can be expected, and there is a need to provide inservice training to deal with them. Most problems can be predicted from other experiences in desegregation. One of the better approaches is to engage in a needs assessment by examining teachers' attitudes on the above items. Many consultants are available to assist in the needs assessment phase. A call to a university should produce someone capable. The needs assessment can give a more clear direction about the problem areas the inservice program should focus on.

The inservice program for staff should be well planned and evaluated.

Much of the school inservice activity over the years has been poorly planned and not as effective as it should or could have been. Planning should be done with outside professional help. In many states, help is available from either state departments of education or from Title IV funded General Assistance Centers.[7] A contact with the state education department ought to give the direction needed.

Because inservice training is trying to make major change in behaviors, it is important that activities be carried on by professional trainers who have had a large amount of experience. The training should also be evaluated carefully to see if it is making the impact it was designed to make.

ESAA funding is available for this inservice training. Funds must be applied for and are awarded on a competitive basis. School districts with great need are usually given funding, however.

FUNDING FOR DESEGREGATION

The planning and implementation of a desegregation plan is expensive. If there are major changes to be made, such as the closing of buildings or erection of new buildings, the addition of certain curricular offerings, the changing of the grade structure, the inservicing of staff, the preparation of community, the hiring of additional staff, or the transportation of students, costs can be very high. For large school districts costs can run into millions of dollars, and some recurring costs become permanent expenditures. These costs must be borne by the district unless there are other places where the money can be acquired.

Costs for transportation can be shared by the state board of education and the school district. Most state departments of education have some funding procedure by which they pay a portion of the cost of purchase of vehicles and the cost of daily transportation. It is important to calculate this ahead of time so that one can know who will pay what part of transportation costs.

The cost of everything else, with the exception of the inservice training of staff and community, is usually borne by the district, but some avenues are available for assistance. Planning may be partially paid for by assistance from a General Assistance Center. Litigation costs are always borne by the district. If the court sees fit to do so, it can order that other costs be shared by the state. These orders are usually challenged by the state; however, it is possible that more money might be forthcoming in the future as local schools are having difficulty securing the money necessary for desegregation. It is usually worth the effort to attempt to get the state to share the costs.

The inservice activities for both staff and community can be paid for from Emergency School Assistance Act funds. The ESAA was passed in 1974, and the funds available are expressly for the purpose of assisting in paying costs of activities that are imminent because of desegregation, but not for the implementation of the court-ordered plan. ESAA will pay for correcting certain educational deficiencies found in children in desegregated situations and will pay for programs affecting student attitudes. ESAA guidelines for funding and requests for proposal are available in September with deadlines for proposal submission set in November or December. The funding period is for one year, after which another proposal must be submitted. Programs are carefully monitored by federal program officers. State departments of education have all the information necessary for securing ESAA funding.

Many school districts have had difficulty getting tax levies for operations passed subsequent to the implementation of court-ordered desegregation plans. When this happens, not much can be done except to continue to go back to the public and ask them for support. The state legislature must be constantly made aware of the difficulties that a school district may be having. The provision for educational activities is a state constitutional guarantee; therefore, when a school district is in financial trouble, the state should share the burden.

The planning for implementing desegregation must begin long before the plan has been completed. When the court orders a plan to be put into operation at a certain date, the board of education, administrators, and teachers must know exactly what they are to do. Planners must keep in mind that a successful desegregation activity largely depends on the school district's staff and citizens' abilities to cope with changes inherent in the plan. The court will not often ask for a specific plan for implementation, but planners must not lose sight of the importance of one.

The court order must be drawn in a way that gives the school district explicit direction in implementation. The order should not immobilize a school district financially. The order should direct other political entities to participate in the funding; it should not direct that the school district pay for activities that could be paid for from other sources. The order should also establish a citizen's monitoring committee and give it clear directions as to its role in seeing that the order is followed and the plan implemented.

The school officials should keep the public informed on issues related to the desegregation plan. Information disseminated quickly and accurately will help control rumors, which are a natural part of change. The public must also take an active part in seeing that problems are handled, and people are informed. Political, school, and governmental leaders should take a positive stance on desegregation and provide leadership that will keep problems under control rather than excite the citizenry through ill-informed statements.

Strong, well-planned inservice programs should be mounted for teachers, administrators, parents, and students. These programs should focus on the needs identified for that community. These programs should be evaluated to see if they are meeting their objectives.

Finally, all available local, state, and federal funding sources must be contacted and asked for resources. The dollar cost of desegregation is high, and the school district should get as much help as it can to ensure a successful implementation.

SELECTED COURT DECISIONS

Brinkman v. *Gilligan,* 503 F.2d 684, 704 (6th Cir. 1974).

Cisneros v. *Corpus Christi Independent School District,* 467 F.2d 142 (1972).

Cooper v. *Aaron* (Ark.) 78 S.Ct. 1401, 358 U.S. 1, 3 L.Ed.2d 5, 19 (1958).

Randall v. *Sumter School District* (S.C.) 1964.

Wright v. *Council of City of Emporia* (Va.) 92 S.Ct. 2196, 407 U.S. 451, 33 L.Ed.2d 51 (1972).

SELECTED BIBLIOGRAPHY

Bash, James H. *Effective Teaching in the Desegregated School.* Bloomington, Ind.: Phi Delta Kappa Educational Foundation, 1976.

Carol, Lila N. "Court-Mandated Citizen Participation in School Desegregation." *Phi Delta Kappan* 59, no. 3 (November 1977): 171–173.

Forehand, G. A.; M. Ragosta; and D. A. Rock. *Conditions and Procedures for Effective School Desegregation. Final Technical Report for U.S. Office of Education.* Contract OEC–0–73–6341. Princeton, N.J.: Educational Testing Service, 1976. (ED 131–155)

Forehand, G. A.; and M. Ragosta. *A Handbook for Integrated Schooling.* Contract OEC–0–73–6341. Princeton, N.J.: Educational Testing Service, 1976. (ED 131–155)

Gordon, Edmund W. *A Comparative Study of Quality Integrated Education. Final Report for National Institute of Education.* Grant N.E.G. 00–3–0156, Project 3–1495. New York: Institute for Urban and Minority Education, Teacher's College, Columbia University, 1976. (ED 128–546)

Hughes, Larry W. *Informal and Formal Community Forces: External Influences on Schools and Teachers.* Morristown, N.J.: General Learning Press. 1976.

Hughes, Larry W., and William M. Gordon. "Frontiers of Law." In *The Courts and Education. Seventy-Seventh Yearbook of the National Society for the Study of Education.* Chicago: University of Chicago Press, 1978. Chapter 13.

Levine, Daniel U., and Robert Havinghurst, eds. *The Future of Big City Schools.* Berkeley, Calif.: McDurken, 1977.

Love, Barbara J. "Desegregation in Your School: Behavior Patterns That Get in the Way." *Phi Delta Kappan* 59, no. 3 (November 1977): 168–170.

Pettigrew, T. F. *A Study of School Integration.* Cooperative Research Project 6–1774, Cambridge Mass.: Harvard University Press 1970.

U.S. Civil Rights Commission. *Desegregation in the Nations Schools.* Washington, D.C.: The Commission, August 1976.

NOTES

1. Carol Lilan, "Court-Mandated Citizen Participation in School Desegregation," *Phi Delta Kappan* 59, no. 3 (November 1977): 172

2. Ibid., p. 173.

3. In *Bradley* v. *Milliken*, Judge DeMascio ordered the Michigan Board of Education to pay part of the costs for implementing the Detroit desegregation plan.

4. *Fulfilling the Letter and Spirit of the Law: Desegregation of the Nation's Public Schools. A Report of the U.S. Commission on Civil Rights* (Washington, D.C.: The Commission, August 1976).

5. Larry W. Hughes, *Informal and Formal Community Forces: External Influences on Schools and Teachers.* (Morristown, N.J.: General Learning Press, 1976), p. 15.

6. Barbara J. Love, "*Desegregation in Your School: Behavior Patterns That Get in the Way,*" *Phi Delta Kappan* 59, no. 3 (November 1977): 168–170.

7. General Assistance Centers are funded under Title IV of the Civil Rights Act of 1964. They are located at major universities in many states.

11

Second-Generation Desegregation Problems

In chapter 2, we drew a distinction between *desegregation* and *integration*. The distinction is a real one, and administrators in school districts that have recently desegregated schools soon realize how clear the distinction is. Social acceptance and better education do not automatically occur by causing a school to be composed of students from different races or ethnic backgrounds. The problem may be further compounded when the student body also reflects wide diversity in socioeconomic levels.

Unless there is conscious, sensitive planning, the recently desegregated school is frequently characterized by student (and faculty) hostility, resentment, and an inadequate administrative response system. It is a school in which neither staff nor students accept one another, and ultimate resegregation is a likely possibility.

This chapter is divided into three parts. The first part describes frequent occurrences in recently desegregated schools. Then we detail an approach for analyzing what is taking place. A discussion of potential problem areas focuses on educational programs, co-curricular activities, and the school climate. The last part of the chapter identifies strategies that can be employed to mitigate or avoid second-generation desegregation problems. We present two helpful questionnaires to be used with the professional staff. The questionnaires identify desirable practices and provide suggestions for active programs.

AFTER THE BODIES ARE MIXED

Court-ordered or otherwise, the desegregation plan is implemented, and students who heretofore lived in single-race or ethnic school environments are faced with a new experience. The more mature students bring with them old loyalties and attitudes, and whether the move to desegregation was rancorous or not, not a little anxiety. Even younger students have been privy to family dinner-table conversation, and they are not immune to pronouncements of peers, friends, and perhaps some less than supportive "others" in the community.

Desegregation plan implementation is frequently traumatic; for many communities, it is a dramatic shift in public policy, and change is always traumatic. Issues surrounding desegregation have been around for so many years that it would be curious indeed to find someone, young or old who did not have a position to express. The first days and months of plan implementation tend to be characterized by tension.

The tension is felt not only by students and parents. Teachers, administrators, and other school personnel frequently feel caught up in a web of anxiety and a fear of the unknown secondary consequences of what often is a significant reorganization of the school. The professional and popular literature abounds with horror stories and success stories, but little of an analytic or prescriptive nature is available. Too many "Louisville–Jefferson County incidents" have taken their toll, and the effects of first-generation desegregation problems, real or imagined, are felt.

First-generation desegregation problems are notable for the hostile reaction of some people in a given school district to the process of desegregation, that is, to the intended assignment of children of different races or ethnic backgrounds to the same schools. These first-generation problems often can be sensational and tragic. They may involve, for example, the harassment of children assigned to formerly all-white schools. Sometimes this harassment goes so far as to place children in physical danger.

More or less violent actions may have taken place in the community at large. There may have been mass meetings to "do something" about the "calamity" that is occurring. First-generation desegregation problems are very apparent because they involve obviously negative and sometimes violent acts on the part of those who object to the reassignment of students. Violent actions, if they take place, are likely to occur in a community during the first months of desegregation.

Frequently there is a collective sigh of relief as the decision to desegregate is made and the plan is finally implemented. And, if the first days and months are unmarred by organized resistance, a deceiving quiet may settle on the school. Yet the basis for second-generation desegregation problems may be forming.

Second-generation problems are much different from first-generation ones. Consider the following description, taken from a case study in a recently published book about the secondary school principalship.

A Developing Problem

The principal of a recently desegregated high school has lately begun to feel that, while there is little apparent overt hostility, the school may be in for some troubling times. Several things lead to this conclusion.

Student interaction is almost totally within racial and ethnic groups. Social groupings in the cafeteria, halls, and at school sponsored events reveal this condition.

Teachers comment that similar interaction patterns exist in the classroom, and some end their comments with a statement like, *"They* just don't seem to fit in well." (This same general lack of social interaction among faculty members who represent different racial and ethnic backgrounds is noticeable as well.)

Moreover, except for some of the boys' athletic teams, there seems to be little minority participation in school activities. Even athletic participation is limited to junior varsity and varsity sports programs; few minority youth participate in the after-school intramural program. School dances, too, reveal remarkable separatism. One ethnic group hardly participates at all and some members of the racial minority have come to you requesting that there be two spring dances held because the band selected for the annual prom by the student prom committee "doesn't play the right kind of music and so why can't we have one of our own?"

Obvious too, after a cursory review of student records and teacher grade sheets, is that grades received appear to be significantly different between racial and ethnic groups. It is true, too, that certain curricula and certain courses reflect racial or ethnic separation. Attendance, truancy, and drop out rates also seem to reflect racial and ethnic differences, as do reports of disciplinary action.

Attendance at school open houses and at meetings of the struggling parent-teacher organization is primarily by the majority racial and ethnic group. Almost no minority group parents or students sign up for the regularly scheduled "rap" sessions.

It seems that the student body may be "mixed" insofar as total reporting is concerned but nothing approximating an integrated school setting exists. Professional conferences and conversations with other principals reveal that if these conditions continue to be unmitigated a strong possibility exists for severe interruption of the learning process and perhaps considerable conflict and disorder.[1]

This case study describes a common situation. What is uncommon is the effective professional action to anticipate and mitigate the situation. The "second generation" has arrived.

What Can Be Expected?

Unmitigated, the conditions that are described in the case study serve as a portent. Not long ago, one of the authors visited a recently desegregated high school where a former student was an assistant principal. During the visit a near riot involving the students occurred, with the result that a large number of students walked out of school, another large number staged a sit-down strike in the halls, and the rest of the student body was kept in locked classrooms by their teachers.

The situation and its follow-up is described in a letter the author received from the assistant principal. The letter is reproduced here in complete and unedited form. The writer was promised that the names of the school and certain individuals would not be revealed.

Dear Dr. Hughes:

I promised to write you a letter at the conclusion of the incident which you witnessed during your recent visit in our school. However, if I wait till the conclusion it might be sometime before I would answer your letter. Therefore, let me bring you up to date on what has occurred since you left.

On the Monday following the sit-down which you witnessed we began a series of conferences with small groups of students (15–20) attempting to pinpoint the grievances of the student body as a whole. These conferences continued for three days with most of the major grievances eventually being brought to our attention.

On Thursday of the next week we scheduled an assembly, at which time the administration was to air and respond to the grievances which had been identified. We were also to have a roving microphone for the students to ask questions of the administration. The questions were to be of a general nature and apply to the student body as a whole.

From the outset the assembly was probably doomed to failure in that the students segregated themselves on opposite sides of the gym like two alien armies facing each other. Even at that the assembly progressed smoothly until the final five minutes before dismissal. At that point a white girl took the microphone and proceeded to verbally degrade the bulletin boards that the black students had put up in honor of National Negro History Week. Mr. X, our principal, defended the right of any group in the school to use the bulletin boards, upon request, to express a view, opinion, or give recognition. Although aroused, this seemed to satisfy the black students momentarily until the next white student took the microphone and continued in the same train of thought. His exact statement was: "If the blacks wanted to honor someone in their history they should have honored Abraham Lincoln, because he was the one who freed the slaves." With that statement the blacks exploded, arose in mass, and walked out of the gym to the applause of the white students. The bell rang for dismissal at that time and the white students began to leave only to be attacked all over the school grounds by roving bands of blacks, both boys and girls.

If you've never been through an experience of that nature no amount of words can describe the totally helpless despair that runs through your mind. It seemed like a horrible nightmare. This can't be happening to us after all our efforts in the opposite direction. Kids were running everywhere, girls screaming and crying, bloody noses, angry exchanges, teachers and staff members futilely attempting to put children on buses. We finally got the majority of kids on the buses and off the school grounds. The police had been called, but did not arrive until after the buses were on their way off the grounds. Fortunately no one was seriously injured, although there were numerous cuts, bruises, bloody noses and slapped faces.

It was the purpose of the board and superintendent to keep the school open if at all possible. We began the day on Friday morning with a contingent of 25 police and detectives in the building to maintain order and only about one-half of our enrollment in attendance.

As a result of Thursday afternoon we had decided that the scheduled assembly for Friday afternoon in honor of Black History Week should be cancelled. Even with the police in presence it was practically impossible to obtain any order when the blacks learned that "Their" assembly had been cancelled. After much debate and pleading by the faculty sponsor of the assembly, we decided to go ahead with the assembly on a voluntary basis. Many white students signed out of school and went home. The mood of the school settled to an uneasy calm awaiting the start of the assembly. To insure further security a large contingent of State Highway Patrol was brought in prior to the assembly. The assembly went off without any trouble and I really regret that more of our student body did not participate. In spite of its controversial nature, it was an imaginative and interesting program. To our sigh of relief, the students dismissed and went home.

On Monday morning of this week we returned to work with eight policemen, one detective and one captain indefinitely assigned to our school. Also over the weekend the board of trustees adopted a very hard-nosed disciplinary code making practically every form of disobedience a suspension or expulsion offense.

We have spent the major part of this week identifying and administering appropriate disciplinary action to those directly involved in last week's disruption. We are also taking a very hard-nose attitude toward any other infractions this week. I'm not sure at this point whether I agree entirely with the philosophy, but I do agree with the board's announced policy to keep the schools open for those who want to seriously pursue an education.

On the positive side we will begin this week a program with a group of consultants from the University of X's Educational Development Center. This is to be a program along the line of some of the work that Dr. X has done with human relations. This will involve our entire faculty in several weeks of inservice in which the students will be dismissed early and we will have several hours of regular school time to conduct the inservice. At a very early interval students will also be involved. This is something that I had asked for as early as last year in anticipation of our desegregated situation this year. It took a long time to convince the "boys upstairs" it was important. It almost seems like "closing the barn door after the horse is gone" at this point. I am sure, however, that there is much to be gained from this group.

I appreciated your visit last week and look forward to seeing you soon.

An electric situation indeed is described by this letter. How did it get that way? The next part of this chapter analyzes the elements and conditions in a newly desegregated environment.

ANALYZING PROBLEMS[2]

To analyze the conditions that cause the second-generation desegregation problems just illustrated, it is necessary to examine three elements of the school environment: the instructional program, co-curricular activities, and the school climate.

The Instructional Program

The desegregated school frequently experiences great stress in the implementation of the instructional program. This is expecially true in the secondary school, but at all levels teachers and administrators often find that pervasive instructional problems, which occur in schools everywhere, desegregated or not, seem to be compounded in the desegregated school. Venditti[3] cites two reasons for this: (1) Often, minority-group students have had limited educational opportunities. The sad fact is that they probably attended schools that were not, by any measure, as good as the schools majority youngsters attended.[4] (2) Tensions and hostility, and feelings of insecurity and fear, which seem to permeate a newly desegregated school, create an atmosphere that is counter to a good learning climate for both minority and majority groups.

An outcome of the first factor may be to develop rigidly tracked curriculums based on ability grouping or test scores, the net effect of which will be resegregation by class within the school. Aside from their dubious educational value, such practices engender further resentment from minority students, their parents, and other interested parties. An outcome of the second factor may be a wary truce, sporadic fights, and resegregation into identifiable social groupings in the school. In neither instance is the basic reason for desegregation furthered.

Institutional racism. There is incipient institutional racism in the desegregated school. Institutional racism, by definition, is composed of those factors and organizational practices, procedures, and rules, not necessarily conscious, that keep certain groups of people in an inferior status not because they are of that specific group but because of the effects of the accepted practices. For example, a regulation requiring that members of the girls' drill team wear their hair at shoulder length will automatically keep many black girls from participating, although the rule is not overtly racist. Similarly, high laboratory fees, while seemingly necessary, will keep economically deprived students from participating in certain academic courses.[5]

Ability grouping serves as yet another example. Frequently, for what appears to be the best of reasons, a practice will be introduced that has the effect of producing institutional racism.

Co-Curricular Activities

> ... the desegregated school ... is once again markedly distinguishable in a most unfortunate way. One finds that extra class activities are largely the province of majority group students. Participation of minority group students on athletic teams may present somewhat of an exception but even in this sphere there are likely to be anomalies. [Some sports may seem to be reserved primarily for one group.][6]

It is also true that many common school practices exclude students on a socioeconomic basis.[7]

Some reasons for the exclusion of large numbers of students in certain athletic programs are the following: standards for cheerleaders and majorettes are often based on skill training given at paid clinics; selection procedures for cheerleaders and majorettes are such that majority-group members frequently make the critical choices; students must purchase uniforms, school symbols, and mascots; students must finance trips; and there are arbitrary quota systems. In activities related to student government there are such inhibiting factors as methods of election, eligibility requirements, faculty approval, and arbitrary quota systems. In activities relating to school- or grade-wide social events, the following can be noted: negative attitudes of the general community and staff about integrated dances, proms, and the expenses connected with such activities. Even the physical location of certain events is often inhibiting. For example, proms tend to exclude minority students when they are held at places far from the home community.

As for activities related to academic and special-interest groups, yet another set of factors tends to exclude some students. These factors relate directly to the previous orientation and background of the children. In a desegregated school, there may be an FAA chapter, a Key Club, or a Chess Club, but there may not be a Soul Music Club or a Black Heritage Club. Moreover, sponsor attitudes and selective recruitment procedures may be a further deterrent to a student's participation in academic and special-interest activities.[8]

School Climate

Permeating the atmosphere of the newly desegregated school are the attitudes, fears, anxieties, and perceptions of students, teachers, and administrators. In combination with all the factors previously discussed, these become the school climate. Some schools, not necessarily desegrated ones, are "uptight places," but the basis for an unproductive school climate may be even more prevalent in desegregated schools.

> The desegregated school, first of all, is a place where the majority race dominates the life of the school. It establishes and maintains the social system and sets the intellectual climate, the dress, values, and behavioral codes of the school. The members of the majority race are a part of the mainstream of life in the school and obtain substantial rewards in the form of privileges, prerogatives, status, and material symbols. By contrast and by definition members of the minority group are outside the mainstream and away from its benefits.[9]

The quotation is from a white director of a federally funded desegregation center. His view is shared by minorities, as reported in an inquiry conducted in the Dallas independent school district.

> The black/Mexican-American view concludes that the Anglo majority has to deal with both a minority school system and with their own value system, i.e., conservative, business-oriented views. Their perceptions of reality led them to make a few changes that would eliminate the more obvious problems but at the same time maintain the present power structure. That delicate balance was looked upon with disfavor by those minorities who perceived that additional basic changes were needed.[10]

A school with a climate characterized by these two reports will find much biracial or ethnic separation. When one group perceives itself as an "invader," and another group sees itself as "threatened," it is not surprising to find conspicuous separation and little social interaction.[11] Manifestations of this climate will be the informal maintenance of separate eating areas in the cafeteria, social-group clustering in the corridors throughout the school day, and the not infrequent informal establishment of certain areas of the building as "home turf."

In a desegregated school characterized by this atmosphere, the kind of situation described in the letter by the assistant principal can be expected to occur. Complaints about a "double standard" will be heard from both groups. The majority group may say that standards for behavior and scholastic performance are being lowered to benefit the minority and that *"they are allowed to get away with everything."* On the other hand, minority-group members may state that they are unduly punished, that unreasonable expectations are being maintained, and they may cite such things as a higher than usual suspension and expulsion rate for their group members as suggestive of inequity. Both groups may be right (or wrong)! Teacher and administrator behavior in such a school often reflects uncertainty and vacillates from situation to situation.

One final analytical point needs to be made. In the desegregated school the racial or ethnic segregation that can be observed among students may also occur among faculty members, and must be guarded against. Teachers and administrators may unconsciously demonstrate an adult brand of voluntary separatism. Students respond to their environment and what they observe to be the normative social behavior of adults. Faculty members need to be conscious of their role as models.[12]

IDENTIFYING AND ADDRESSING PROBLEMS

Sensitive and sensible preparation and manifest behavior on the part of the professional staff will result in the anticipation and mitigation, if not the total resolution, of potential second-generation desegregation problems. In their very important book, *A Handbook for Integrated Schooling,*[13] Forehand and Ragosta establish an effective integrated school as being characterized by four distinguishing features:

1. *Salience.* Successful integration is a highly salient goal for most people in effective schools, and for the most influential people in a school. Salience has both motivational and perceptual components. Motivationally, successful integration needs to be an important goal, internalized by both staff and students. It must take a high position among the myriad goals that a school must have. Perceptually, there must be a high degree of attentiveness to progress in integration and alertness to indications of success and failure.

Salience implies absence of racially prejudiced behavior. The association of lack of prejudice on the part of the staff and positive attitudes on the part of students is one of the most pervasive findings in our study. Absence of racial prejudice on the part of the school staff is an important goal. Even if attitude change is not achieved for every staff member, a professional attitude that minimizes prejudiced behavior can be demanded. Salience also implies intention to act positively to achieve good race relations. Such intention may be motivated by a professional attitude and dedication to duty. It need not imply any particular political or ideological position.

2. *Intercultural Sensitivity.* People in effective schools are sensitive to the cultural backgrounds of the students, to the effect of backgrounds on behavior, self-concept, and aspirations, and to the need to design and carry out educational programs responsively.

3. *Interdependence.* Many respondents in effective schools often used the term "school family." It implies shared objectives, mutual concern, and mutual sensitivity. Members of a successful school family include the administration, faculty, and students. In successful schools, family feeling is regarded as desirable and rewarding.

4. *Equity.* In successful schools, the races and individual members of races are treated equitably. The term equity implies fairness and justice. It is neither synonymous with nor antithetical to equality. A school may provide equal opportunity to participate in its activities—in the sense that the activities are open to all—yet without establishing equity. If geographic location, cultural tradition, or minority status are barriers to equal participation, the mere absence of school-imposed barriers does not constitute equity. If minority students must work harder because of a heavier burden of transportation, or need to overcome negative expectations, or informal discrimination, the effect is inequity. The establishment of equity in a school requires positive action. Passively administered policies of equality are not enough.[14]

The Discrepancy Analysis

How does a school react? A discrepancy analysis in which all faculty members participate is necessary for two reasons. First, such an analysis will have as one product a raised level of awareness on the part of faculty members about the many facets of an effectively integrated school, and it will point out needed areas of personal improvement. Second, and equally if not more important, the analysis will point out where the current operating level is in relation to practices essential to a successfully desegregated school.

The discrepancy analysis begins with information gathering about what is currently occurring in the school. We suggest using the elementary school and high school diagnostic questionnaires developed by Forehand and Ragosta.[15] These questionnaires are not only diagnostic but prescriptive, and thus they are invaluable to a school faculty and community that desires high-quality integrated education.

Eight parts make up the elementary school questionnaire shown as figure 11.1. They focus on

1. The degree to which the curriculum of the school reflects multiethnicity

2. The nature of the co-curriculur activities program and the attention to the fact that many students do not live close by

3. The way students are grouped for instruction

4. Multiethnic teaching practices including the openness with which racial differences are treated

5. The quality of home-school relations

6. The nature of existing rules and regulations and the modes of disciplinary actions taken

7. The degree to which staffing patterns reflect true integration

8. The principal's leadership behavior

Answers to questions within each category will provide the substance for necessary corrective or pro-active adjustments in the operation of the school. A similar questionnaire should be distributed to students and community members because perceptions often vary. If this is true on any particular item or in any category, that issue will need to be addressed. Perceptions determine behavior.

FIGURE 11.1

Elementary School Diagnostic Questions

Topic: *The Multiethnic Curriculum*

Do primers and readers contain minority characters? Yes ___ No ___

Do primers and readers portray situations in which minority characters have equal status roles with the majority? Yes ___ No ___

Do social studies texts contain information about black leaders and black people? Yes ___ No ___

Do American history textbooks cover black Americans? Yes ___ No ___

Does the music curriculum—or chorus and band—cover the music of black people? Yes ___ No ___

Does the library contain books and materials dealing with black history and culture and the contributions of black Americans? Yes ___ No ___

Does the school have a plan to systematically replace old texts such as readers and social studies texts with integrated textbooks? Yes ___ No ___

Have all teachers attended black history or culture courses? Yes ___ No ___

Does the school have a Multiethnic Committee or a Human Relations Committee concerned with the issues of integrated education? Yes ___ No ___

Topic: *Co-curricular Activities*

Does the school program provide for co-curricular activities? Yes ___ No ___

Can students attend co-curricular activities without regard to grades earned? Yes ___ No ___

Are bused students able to attend as readily as nonbused students? Yes ___ No ___

Are co-curricular activities free of cost or free to those who cannot afford to pay? Yes ___ No ___

Topic: *Achievement and Grouping*

Does every class in the school come close to reflecting the ratio of black to white students in the total school? Yes ___ No ___

Where students are assigned to remedial or special education programs which remove them from the mainstream of students, does the referral system provide for the consensus of several professionals? Yes ___ No ___

Does every student spend a large part of the school day in challenging courses of study? Yes ___ No ___

Does every student have the opportunity for positive interracial contact with equal status? Yes ___ No ___

Topic: *Multiethnic Teaching*

Do administrators and teachers discuss race openly in faculty meetings? Yes ___ No ___

Have there been any assemblies which dealt with race? — Yes ___ No ___

Do teachers discuss race with students in the classroom? — Yes ___ No ___

Do teachers make assignments such that black and white students work together? — Yes ___ No ___

Do teachers praise all students for their accomplishments rather than praising only those who accomplish the most? — Yes ___ No ___

Are teachers equally friendly with their black students and their white students? — Yes ___ No ___

Do teachers try to avoid warning or blaming students and scolding them for misbehavior? — Yes ___ No ___

Do students spend the major part of the school day involved in learning? — Yes ___ No ___

Topic: *Home and School*

Do teachers know the parents of their students? — Yes ___ No ___

Have all parents visited the school? — Yes ___ No ___

Do as many black parents attend school functions as white parents? — Yes ___ No ___

Have teachers attempted to find out what barriers keep parents from involvement in school activities? — Yes ___ No ___

Is there a parent organization in the school? — Yes ___ No ___

Does the parent organization have a membership representative of all major racial or ethnic groups in the school? — Yes ___ No ___

Do black and white parents have equal status in the parent organization? — Yes ___ No ___

Do teachers visit the homes of parents who cannot get to the school? — Yes ___ No ___

Does the school have an even-handed policy for handling parent requests such as changing students' classroom assignments because of the race of the teacher? — Yes ___ No ___

Where community opposition to integration exists, have black and white parents been involved in helping to develop a school policy on racial issues? — Yes ___ No ___

Topic: *Rules and Discipline*

Are white students equally likely to be punished for breaking the rule as black students? — Yes ___ No ___

Are the rules perceived to be fair by black and white teachers and students? — Yes ___ No ___

Is the general reaction to student misbehavior rational rather than emotional? — Yes ___ No ___

Are students who disobey rules helped to understand the reasons for the rule and guided toward improved behavior? — Yes ___ No ___

Have teachers and administrators discussed rules and discipline together? — Yes ___ No ___

Is there general agreement among the faculty as to disciplinary procedure? — Yes ___ No ___

Topic: *Staffing*

Is the faculty integrated? — Yes ___ No ___

Does it generally reflect the racial composition of the students in the school? — Yes ___ No ___

Do black and white personnel at the school have equal status? — Yes ___ No ___

Topic.: *Principal's Leadership*

Has the principal articulated the goals of the school? — Yes ___ No ___

Do teachers know the goals of the school? — Yes ___ No ___

Do those goals include good academic achievement? — Yes ___ No ___

Do the goals include good race relations? — Yes ___ No ___

Is there a strong planning and evaluation component built into faculty meetings? — Yes ___ No ___

Is there time set aside for the principal and teachers to discuss
problems together?   Yes ___   No ___
Are discussions of problems action-oriented, i.e., is the major
emphasis on finding alternative solutions?   Yes ___   No ___

SOURCE: Garlie A. Forehand and Majorie Ragosta, *A Handbook for Integrated Schooling*
(Princeton, N.J.: Educational Testing Service, 1976). Reprinted by permission.

The high school questionnaire is similar but not identical to the elementary school questionnaire. Because of the relatively more complex organizational arrangements in high schools, some categories contain additional
questions, and the categories are not all the same as those in the elementary
questionnaire. A brief description of the categories follows:

1. *The multi-ethnic curriculum* category focuses on all aspects of the high school
    curriculum: subject-matter courses, fine arts, and library materials.

2. *Co-curricular activities* include provision for those students who live long dis-
    tances from the school.

3. *Multiethnic teaching* questions focus on teacher-student interactions and
    classroom organization.

4. *The quality of home-school relations* is obvious.

5. *Rules and discipline.* Here, in addition to the substance and application of
    rules, attention is directed to the way in which the rules were developed.

6. *Staffing composition and patterns* examine the degree of staff integration. At-
    tention is directed as well to committee organization, including provision for
    a human relations committee.

7. *Student personnel* focus is on the establishment and composition of a student
    human relations organization. Also examined are the roles and responsibili-
    ties of such a group.

8. *Internal integration* is the final category on the high school questionnaire. This
    focuses on the degree to which all aspects of student life are desegregated.

FIGURE 11.2

High School Diagnostic Questions

Topic: *The Multiethnic Curriculum*

Does the required English curriculum include study of black
authors?   Yes ___   No ___
Are there literature courses available that emphasize the
contributions of minority-group authors?   Yes ___   No ___
Do courses in American history present accomplishments and
contributions of black Americans?   Yes ___   No ___
Do social studies courses deal with African, Asian, American Indian,
and Latin American cultures, as well as European?   Yes ___   No ___
Are there elective social studies courses available that emphasize the
contributions of nonwhite people and cultures?   Yes ___   No ___
Do fine arts courses reflect contributions of nonwhite artists and
cultures?   Yes ___   No ___
Does the music curriculum—or chorus and band—cover the music of
black people?   Yes ___   No ___

Does the library contain books and materials dealing with black history and culture and the contributions of black Americans?   Yes ___ No ___

Does the school have a systematic plan to replace old texts with integrated textbooks?   Yes ___ No ___

Have all teachers attended black history or culture courses?   Yes ___ No ___

Is material dealing with minority and majority groups presented in a manner that is integrated from both a logical and social point of view?   Yes ___ No ___

Are minority-group members portrayed in a manner that is free of stereotypes?   Yes ___ No ___

Topic: *Co-curricular Activities*

Can students attend co-curricular activities without regard to grades earned?   Yes ___ No ___

Are bused students able to attend as readily as nonbused students?   Yes ___ No ___

Are co-curricular activities free of cost or free to those who cannot afford to pay?   Yes ___ No ___

Topic: *Multiethnic Teaching*

Have there been any assemblies which dealt with race?   Yes ___ No ___

Do teachers discuss race with students in the classroom?   Yes ___ No ___

Do teachers make assignments so that black and white students work together?   Yes ___ No ___

Do teachers praise all students for their accomplishments rather than praise only those who accomplish the most?   Yes ___ No ___

Are teachers equally friendly with their black students and their white students?   Yes ___ No ___

Do teachers try to avoid warning or blaming students and scolding them for misbehavior?   Yes ___ No ___

Do students spend the major part of the school day involved in learning?   Yes ___ No ___

Topic: *Home and School*

Have all parents visited the school?   Yes ___ No ___

Do as many black parents attend school functions as white parents?   Yes ___ No ___

Has the school attempted to find out what barriers keep parents from involvement in school activities?   Yes ___ No ___

Is there a parent organization in the school?   Yes ___ No ___

Does the parent organization have a membership representative of all major racial or ethnic groups in the school?   Yes ___ No ___

Do black and white parents have equal status in the parent organization?   Yes ___ No ___

Where community opposition to integration exists, have black and white parents been involved in helping to develop a school policy on racial issues?   Yes ___ No ___

Topic: *Rules and Discipline*

Is there an official school policy on rules and discipline?   Yes ___ No ___

Are all faculty, staff, and students aware of the school rules and the consequences for breaking them?   Yes ___ No ___

Have black students and white students participated in the formulation of school rules and codes of conduct?   Yes ___ No ___

Are the rules perceived to be fair by black and white teachers and students?   Yes ___ No ___

Is the general reaction to student misbehavior rational rather than emotional?   Yes ___ No ___

Have teachers and administrators discussed rules and discipline together?   Yes ___ No ___

Is there general agreement among the faculty as to disciplinary
procedure?   Yes ___ No ___

Topic: *The Staff*

Is the faculty integrated?   Yes ___ No ___
Do black and white personnel at the school have equal status?   Yes ___ No ___
Has the principal articulated the goals of the school?   Yes ___ No ___
Does the staff know the goals of the school?   Yes ___ No ___
Do those goals include good academic achievement?   Yes ___ No ___
Do the goals include good race relations?   Yes ___ No ___
Is there time set aside for the administration and faculty to discuss
race relations and racial issues?   Yes ___ No ___
Do administration and faculty discuss race openly?   Yes ___ No ___
Does the school have a faculty Human Relations Committee or
Multiethnic Committee concerned with the issues of integrated
education?   Yes ___ No ___

Topic: *The Students*

Is there a student group with responsibility for human relations,
including interethnic relations?   Yes ___ No ___
Are members of that group selected by the students?   Yes ___ No ___
Do minorities have equal representation in the human relations
groups?   Yes ___ No ___
Do the functions of the human relations groups include:
    general communication involving minority and majority students?   Yes ___ No ___
    grievance procedures?   Yes ___ No ___
    crisis prevention activities?   Yes ___ No ___
    general problem solving?   Yes ___ No ___
    planning and sponsoring social events?   Yes ___ No ___
    orientation of new students?   Yes ___ No ___
Have the roles, responsibilities, and decision-making powers of the
human relations groups been agreed upon by the administration and
the students?   Yes ___ No ___

Topic: *Internal Integration*

Is there black student and white student representation in all
curriculum tracks, including college preparatory?   Yes ___ No ___
Are all required classes integrated?   Yes ___ No ___
Are most elective classes integrated?   Yes ___ No ___
Where students are assigned to remedial or special education
programs that remove them from the mainstream of students, does
the referral system provide for the census of several professionals?   Yes ___ No ___
Does every student spend a large part of the school day in a
challenging course of study?   Yes ___ No ___
Does every student have the opportunity for positive interracial
contact with equal status?   Yes ___ No ___
Do pictures in school publications generally reflect the racial
composition of the school?   Yes ___ No ___
Are both black and white students represented in the following:
    prom queens and their courts?   Yes ___ No ___
    officers in student government?   Yes ___ No ___
    sport teams?   Yes ___ No ___
    clubs?   Yes ___ No ___
    committees?   Yes ___ No ___
    honors?   Yes ___ No ___

SOURCE: Garlie A. Forehand and Marjorie Ragosta. *A Handbook for Integrated Schooling*
(Princeton, N.J.: Educational Testing Service, 1976). Reprinted by permission.

It is interesting to note that the category of "principal leadership" is not included in the high school questionnaire. This is a serious omission because the behavior of the principal, more than the behavior of any other person, determines the tone of the school. The same questions asked about the elementary principal's behavior should become a part of the high school questionnaire.

The questions are worded in such a way that the desirable response is yes. Any negative response is indicative of a potential problem and should become an item for immediate consideration and solution.

This chapter has focused on problems that may occur after the desegregation plan has been implemented. Frequently a sense of finality exists once children of different races and ethnic groups have been placed together in a single school environment. Yet this is not the end of the challenge. Much remains to be done. Social acceptance and a cooperative, productive school environment depend on more than a simple mixing of bodies.

It is important to recognize that segregation can occur within a single school as well as in a school system. Hostilities and a perceived or real difference in treatment intensify in the more intimate setting of a school building.

Methods of analyzing the degree to which a school is integrated are available. In this final chapter we have attempted to describe symptoms and offer benchmarks against which a desegregated school can be measured.

SELECTED BIBLIOGRAPHY

Bash, James H. *Effective Teaching in the Desegregated School.* Fastback 22. Bloomington, Ind.: Phi Delta Kappa Educational Foundation, 1973. 46 pages (pamphlet).

Bazeli, Frank P. "Integrating the Desegregated School." *NASSP Bulletin* 60 (February 1976).

Beck, William W., and Glenn M. Linden, "Anglo and Minority Perceptions of Success in Dallas School Desegregation." *Phi Delta Kappan* 60, no. 5 (January 1979): 378–82.

Crain, Robert, and Rita Mahard. *Desegregation and Black Achievement.* Durham, N.C.: Institute of Policy Sciences and Public Affairs, 1977.

Estes, Nolan. "On Eliminating Institutional Racism." *Phi Delta Kappan* 60, no. 4 (December 1978): 302–3.

Levine, Daniel V. *Models for Integrated Education.* Worthington, Ohio: Charles A. Jones, 1971. 115 pages.

Forehand, Garlie A., and Marjorie Ragosta. *A Handbook for Integrated Schooling.* Contract OEC–0–73–6341, Department of Health, Education, and Welfare. Princeton, N.J.: Educational Testing Service, 1976.

Fullington, Gail. "Soul Brother or Uncle Tom." *Phi Delta Kappan* 57, no. 7 (March 1976): 446–67.

Gordon, Edmund W. *A Comparative Study of Quality Integrated Education.* New

York: Institute for Urban and Minority Education, Teachers College, Columbia University, 1976.

Hughes, Larry W., and Gerald C. Ubben. *The Secondary School Principal in Action: An Executive Handbook*. Boston: Allyn and Bacon, 1980.

Love, Barbara J. "Desegregation in Your School: Behavior Patterns That Get in the Way." *Phi Delta Kappan* 59, no. 3 (November 1977): 168–70.

Metz, Mary Haywood. *Classrooms and Corridors*. Berkeley, Calif.: University of California Press, 1978.

Ornstein, Allan. "IQ Tests and the Culture Issue." *Phi Delta Kappan* 57, no. 6 (February 1976): 403–4.

Venditti, Frederick P. "Second Generation Desegregation Problems." *Educational Catalyst* 8 (Spring 1978): 100–108.

Walters, E. K. and Reginald Young. "Communicating with Minority Public Takes Extra Effort." *Journal of Educational Communication* 2, no. 4 (Fall 1979): 14–16.

NOTES

1. From Larry W. Hughes and Gerald C. Ubben, *The Secondary School Principal's Handbook: Guide to Executive Action*. (Boston: Allyn and Bacon, 1980), p. 15. Reprinted by permission.

2. Appreciation is expressed to Dr. Frederick P. Venditti for his assistance in the preparation of sections of this part of the chapter. Dr. Venditti is director of the General Assistance Center at the University of Tennessee, Knoxville.

3. Frederick P. Venditti, "Second Generation School Desegregation Problems: A Perspective Provided by the Majority-White Secondary School," *Educational Catalyst* 8, no. 2 (Spring 1978): 103.

4. This conclusion is well documented in Morris Weinberg, *Minority Students: A Research Appraisal* (Washington, D.C.: National Institute of Education, 1977).

5. For further examples, see Nolan Estes, "On Eliminating Institutional Racism," *Phi Delta Kappan* 60, no. 4 (December 1978): 302–4; also see William M. Beck and Glenn M. Linden, "Anglo and Minority Perceptions of Success in Dallas School Desegregation," *Phi Delta Kappa* 60, no. 5 (January 1979): 378–82.

6. Venditti, "Second Generation School Desegregation Problems," p. 104.

7. An examination of this phenomenon can be found in Hughes and Ubben, *Secondary School Principal's Handbook: Guide to Executive Action*, chap. 10, "Managing the Co-curriculum Program."

8. Venditti, "Second Generation School Desegregation Problems," pp. 104–5; Estes, "On Eliminating Racism," p. 303.

9. Venditti, "Second Generation School Desegregation Problems," p. 102.

10. Beck and Linden, "Anglo and Minority Perceptions," p. 381.

11. Venditti points out that frequently there develops one "unsettling" (to some) interaction phenomenon. Despite the obvious racial separation maintained generally by the students, there will be some interracial dating, most often between black males and white females. This deviation from the social norm will frequently cause concern and possible disruption, especially from black females and adults in the school community.

12. A good comparison of the desegregated and integrated school appears in F. Bazeli, "Integrating the Desegregated School," *National Association of Secondary School Principal's Bulletin* 60, no. 397 (February 1976): 80–84. See also "Making Desegregation Work," a series of articles in *Phi Delta Kappan* 59, no. 2 (November 1977): 158–73.

13. Garlie A. Forehand and Marjorie Ragosta, *A Handbook for Integrated Schooling* (Princeton N.J.: Educational Testing Service, 1976). This book was prepared under contract to the U.S. Department of Health, Education, and Welfare. Reprinted by permission.

14. Ibid., pp. 10–11.

15. Ibid., pp. 47–51, 83–88.

Appendix A:
An Annotated Chronology of Events and Significant Cases

1849: *Roberts* v. *Boston*
Massachusetts adopts the first state law establishing separate but equal schools. Charles Sumner, attorney for the plaintiff, argues that separate facilities can never be equivalent because of the stigma of caste they impose.

1873: *Washington A. & G. Railway Co.* v. *Brown,* 84 U.S. 445 (17 Wallaces U.S. 445)
"Separate but equal" in federal accommodations is unconstitutional.

1896: *Plessy* v. *Ferguson,* 16 S.Ct. 1138
"Separate but equal" concept upheld in Louisiana for state transportation services. *Roberts* decision cited as a major precedent for the right of the state to require segregation of colored and white persons in public conveyances.

1899: *Cumming* v. *Beard,* 20 S.Ct. 197
"Separate but equal" doctrine upheld by federal courts for state school systems. Upheld decision of a Georgia school board to close its black high school while continuing to offer a high school education to white youths.

1927: *Gong Lum* v. *Rice,* 275 U.S. 78, 85, 86
State officials could determine who was "colored" for the purpose of school desegregation: "The question here is whether a Chinese citizen of the United States is denied equal protection of the laws when he is classed among the colored races and furnished facilities for education equal to that offered to all, whether white, brown, yellow, or black."

1938: *Gaines* v. *Canada,* 342 S.Ct. 121
"Separate but equal" doctrine applies only when all facilities are under one state's authority. In *Pearson* v. *Murray* (169 Md. 478), decided in 1936, the Maryland courts compelled the university law school to admit blacks instead of sending them to out-of-state law schools since (1) the education they received out of state would not be "equal" to that at the University of Maryland, if the individual wished to practice law in Maryland; and (2) the state had not authorized the establishment of a law school within the state for blacks. The *Gaines* case in Missouri accepted the same idea, though it complied by establishing a separate black institution, since the state had authorized its construction.

1940: *Abton* v. *Norfolk School Board,* 61 S.Ct. 75
"Separate but equal" means equal pay for staff even though it be separated; a Virginia court decision.

1944: *Prince* v. *Massachusetts,* 321 U.S. 158

This case involved a conflict between Jehovah's Witnesses and the state. A child of nine years of age and her aunt violated child labor laws by distributing religious pamphlets on the street during the evening. The court decided that "... neither rights of religion nor rights of parenthood are beyond limitation. Acting to guard the general interest in youth's well-being, the State as *parens patriae* may restrict the parent's control by requiring school attendance, regulating or prohibiting the child's labor and in many other ways." The court also stated: "Parents cannot make martyrs of school children for some social issue unless children are old enough to make such a decision."

1954: *Brown* v. *Board of Education of Topeka,* 347 U.S. 483, at 494

Separate schools are "inherently unequal." The court accepted the language of the Kansas district court: "Segregation of white and colored children in public schools has a detrimental effect upon the colored children. The impact is greater when it has the sanction of law; for the policy of separating the races is usually interpreted as denoting the inferiority of the Negro group. A sense of inferiority affects the motivation of a child to learn. Segregation with the sanction of law, therefore, has a tendency to retard the educational and mental development of Negro children and to deprive them of some of the benefits they would receive in a racially integrated school system." The thrust of the case was essentially negative: it prohibited the state from intentionally mandating a dual school system and imposed no affirmative duty on the state to desegregate.

1954: *Gonzales* v. *Sheely,* 96 F.Supp. 1004

This Arizona case involved the segregation of children of Mexican descent in separate school buildings with inferior accommodations and facilities. The court found that the 1954 *Brown* doctrine applied to all ethnic groups.

1954: *Bolling* v. *Sharpe,* 347 U.S. 497

"The *Brown* rules apply to federally supported schools."

1955: *Brown* v. *Board of Education of Topeka,* 349 U.S. 294

"... school authorities have burden of establishing that grant of additional time for transition is necessary in public interest and is consistent with good faith compliance at earliest practicable date." School desegregation must proceed "with all deliberate speed."

1956: *Clemons* v. *Board,* 350 U.S. 1006

Gerrymandering attendance zones in Ohio to maintain segregated schools is unconstitutional.

1957: *New Orleans Board of Education* v. *Bush,* 77 S.Ct. 1380

"State laws supporting segregated schools must give way to federal constitutional mandates."

1957: *Gibson* v. *Board of Public Instruction of Dade County,* 246 F.2d. 913

"Neither Florida Pupil Assignment Law nor any other law could justify violation of Federal Constitution by requiring racial segregation in public schools."

1958: *Cooper* v. *Aaron,* 358 U.S. 1

"Under directive to district courts to require prompt and reasonable start toward desegregation of public schools and to take such action as was necessary to bring about end of racial segregation 'with all deliberate speed,' hostility to racial desegregation would not be justified for not requiring present non-segregated admission of all qualified Negro students."

1961: *Taylor* v. *Board of Education of City School District of City of New Rochelle,* 368 U.S. 940

"Neighborhood school policy is valid only insofar as it is operated within confines established by equal protection clause of Fourteenth Amendment, and it cannot be used as instrument to confine Negroes within area artificially delineated in first instance by official acts." Also, "Decree for desegregation of city schools could not so enshroud rights of Negro pupils with conditions and restrictions as to make sham of court's ruling for desegregation."

1964: *Griffin* v. *County School Board of Prince Edward County,* 377 U.S. 218, at 221

Efforts to desegregate Prince Edward County, Virginia's schools met with resistance. "The General Assembly met in special session and enacted legislation to close any public schools where white and colored children were enrolled together, to cut off state funds to such schools, to pay tuition grants to children in nonsectarian private schools, and to extend state retirement benefits to teachers in newly created private schools." The court decided:. . . "the public schools of Prince Edward County may not be closed to avoid the effect of the law of the land as interpreted by the Supreme Court. . . . "

1966: *Green* v. *County School Board,* 391 U.S. 430

The court was no longer satisfied with state neutrality but charged school officials "with the affirmative duty to make whatever steps might be necessary to convert to a unitary system in which racial discrimination would be eliminated, root and branch." The decision expressed the court's dissatisfaction with a "freedom of choice" plan which had *not* eliminated racially identifiable schools. The school was thus held accountable not only for its positive acts but for acts of omission.

1967: *Alabama State Teacher's Association* v. *Alabama Public School and College Authority,* 393 U.S. 400

Desegregation of schools or colleges must include employees.

1967: *Offermann* v. *Nitkowski,* 378 F.2d.22

"Communities have no constitutional duty to undo bona fide *de facto* school segregation." Also, "Order directing elimination of *de facto* school segregation and local plan adopted pursuant thereto did not violate any constitutional right of complaining parents of white children."

1967: *Hobson* v. *Hansen,* 393 U.S. 801

" '*De jure* school segregation' adverts to specifically mandated by law or by public policy pursued under color of law, and segregation is '*de facto* school segregation' when it results from action of pupil assignment policies not based on race, on social or other conditions for which government cannot be held responsible."

1967: *Clark* v. *Board of Education of Little Rock School District,* 391 U.S. 447

The court stated that the "mere possibility of abuse, or ability of party to envision hypothetical question of constitutional law that may never arise, cannot be used to destroy school desegregation plan that can otherwise be constitutionally applied." Furthermore, the "Constitution does not require a school system to force a mixing of races in school according to some predetermined mathematical formula, and mere presence of statistics indicating absence of total integration does not render an otherwise proper plan unconstitutional."

1967: *U.S.* v. *Jefferson County Board of Education,* 386 U.S. 1001
[The] "necessity of overcoming effects of segregated school system requires integration of faculties, facilities, and activities, as well as students." Also, "When schools are under court-ordered desegregation, courts are responsible for determining sufficiency of system's compliance with decree, and court's task is a continuing process, especially in major areas readily susceptible of observation and measurement, such as faculty integration and student desegregation." And, "Courts should cooperate with Congressional-Executive policy in favor of desegregation and against aiding segregated schools."

1967: *Monroe* v. *Board of Commissioners, City of Jackson, Tennessee,* 390 U.S. 936
"Gerrymandering to preserve segregation in schools is unlawful."

1968: *Green* v. *County School Board of New Ken County,* 391 U.S. 430
"In context of long standing state-imposed segregated public school system, fact that in 1965, school board opened doors of former white school to negro children and a negro school to white children under its 'freedom of choice' plan permitting each pupil to choose school he would attend did not establish that board had taken steps adequate to abolish its dual, segregated system." "Freedom of choice" plan may be allowed to prove itself but "if there are reasonably available other ways, such as zoning, promising speedier and more effective conversion to a unitary, nonracial school system, 'freedom of choice' plan must be held unacceptable."

1968: *Monroe* v. *Board of Commissioners of City of Jackson, Tennessee,* 391 U.S. 450
In Monroe, the court stated that the "school board has affirmative duty to take whatever steps might be necessary to convert to a unitary system in which racial discrimination would be eliminated root and branch." Also, "The key to the legal righteousness of any administrative plan is whether or not it works." The board was directed to "convert promptly to a system without a 'white' school and a 'negro' school, but just schools."

1969: *Singleton* v. *School District* (Mississippi), 419 F. 2d 1211
Delay with the name of deliberation, or deliberate speed, is ended. Desegregation must occur "now"—establish a "unitary" system within the current school year.

1970: *Cisneros* v. *Corpus Christi Independent School District,* 324 F.Supp. 599
"In determining whether a particular group has been unconstitutionally segregated in public school, whether the group represents a numeric minority or a majority of the population in the district is not the controlling inquiry. . . . Also, . . . in determining whether particular school district is unconstitutionally maintaining a dual school system, the relevant determinations are which groups in the school district are underprivileged and politically and economically disadvantaged, and which, if any, of these groups are being unreasonably segregated in the district's school." And, "Desegregation applies to Mexican-American populations as well as Black populations."

1970: *Spangler* v. *Board of Education,* 311 F.Supp. 501, at 524
In *Spangler* it was decided that school officials may recognize race for "noninvidious" discrimination to achieve racial balance. "By requiring that students from two majority black residential areas, the Open District and the Audubon area, be transported to achieve integration, while not transporting children from majority white residential areas to achieve integration, defendants have placed an undue share of the burdens of desegregation on black children and, thus, have violated the Fourteenth Amendment."

1971: *Swann* v. *Charlotte-Mecklenburg Board of Education,* 402 U.S. 1
Swann set the stage for attacks on what was presumed to be *de facto* segregation in the North. The court saw a casual link between past discrimination and the continued existence of segregated schools. The court found that "in a school district where there is a past history of *de jure* segregation, it is the *effect* of decisions made by school officials that is important and not whether these decisions were made with *intent* to maintain segregation." Further, the court stated: "We are concerned in these cases with the elimination of discrimination inherent in the dual school systems, not with myriad factors of human existence which can cause discrimination in a multitude of ways on racial, religious, or ethnic grounds."

At 29 "Bus transportation has been an integral part of the public education system for years, and was perhaps the single most important factor in the transition from the one-room schoolhouse to the consolidated school. Eighteen million of the nation's public school children, approximately 39%, were transported to their schools by bus in 1969–70, in all parts of the country." In default by school authorities of their affirmative obligation to eliminate racial discrimination root and branch, the district courts have broad equitable powers to fashion remedies that will assure unitary school systems. Where there has been legally imposed segregation, it is the responsibility of local authorities and district courts to see to it that future school construction and abandonment are not used and do not serve to perpetuate or reestablish the dual system. The constitutional command to desegregate schools does not mean that every school in every community must *always* reflect the racial composition of the school system as a whole. As interim corrective measure in desegregation cases, altering of attendance zones resulting in zones that are neither compact nor contiguous is within the broad remedial powers of the district courts. Not required to make year-by-year adjustments of racial compositions of student bodies once desegregated. Pairing and grouping of noncontiguous school zones is a permissible desegregation tool; judicial steps in shaping zones going beyond combination of contiguous areas should be examined in the light of the objective, and no rigid rules can be laid down to govern all situations.

1971: *Davis* v. *Board of School Commissioners of Mobile County* (Alabama), 402 U.S. 33
Neighborhood school zoning is not the only constitutionally permissible remedy for segregated school; nor is it per se adequate to meet the remedial responsibility of local boards. The measure of any school desegregation plan is its effectiveness.

1971: *Johnson* v. *San Francisco Unified School District,* 404 U.S. 1215
Johnson spoke to the desegregation of school faculties, experience and qualifications of teachers, and size of classes in predominantly black schools. The district court maintained that the full educational benefits of desegregation could not be achieved by the mere meeting of arithmetical percentages on racial balance. If desegregation was to provide maximum benefit, goodwilled, open-minded, genuine cooperation was needed from the school and community at large.

1971: *Winston-Salem/Forsyth County Board of Education* v. *Scott,* 404 U.S. 1221
Fixed racial balance or quota is not required in desegregation plan.

1972: *Wright* v. *Council of City of Emporia* (Virginia), 407 U.S. 451
"City's proposal to withdraw from participation in county school system which had been found in violation of Constitution must be judged accord-

ing to whether withdrawal hinders or furthers process of school desegregation. Court supervising process of desegregation of school system does not exercise its remedial discretion responsively where it approves plan that, in hope of providing better 'quality education' to some children, has substantial adverse effect on quality of education available to others."

1973: *Soria* v. *Oxnard School District Board of Trustees* (California), 488 F.2d 579
"Hispano and Negroes may be grouped together for the purpose of determining whether a school or school system is unconstitutionally segregated since those groups suffer identical discrimination in treatment when compared with the treatment afforded Anglo students."

1973: *Keyes* v. *School District No. 1,* 413 U.S. 189, 208
Keyes was the first nonsouthern school desegregation case to be heard by the Supreme Court, which declared that "the distinguishing factor between *de facto* and the unlawful *de jure* segregation was the purpose of intent to segregate." As a result of *Keyes,* plaintiffs "must prove not only that segregated schooling exists but also that it was brought about or maintained by intentional state action." *Keyes* is significant, too, in that it allows a plaintiff to effectuate city-wide desegregation with a showing of intentional segregation in only a substantial portion of the school district. The holding indicates the approach that will be taken by the court in dealing with problems of desegregation in a northern context.

1974: *Morgan* v. *Hennigan* (Massachusetts), 379 F.Supp. 410
"Racial hostility is not the applicable standard in determining whether the maintenance of a dual school system is unconstitutional."

1975: *Morgan* v. *Kerrigan* (Massachusetts), 401 F.Supp. 216
"Identifiably one-race schools in a school system inflict two sorts of injury upon minority students, i.e., the affrontery likely to be felt from racial or ethnic isolation, and the cutting off from majority culture which is widely reflected in the standards which determine success in society, of minority students."

1974: *Bradley* v. *School Board, City of Richmond* (Virginia), 416 U.S. 696
This case affirmed the decision of the Fourth Circuit Court of Appeals in which the trial court order for the creation of a "superdistrict" for the metropolitan area was reversed.

1974: *Higgins* v. *Board of Education of Grand Rapids* (Michigan), 395 F.Supp. 444, aff'd 508 F.2d 779
"Changes of school district boundary lines and feeder patterns would not support charges of gerrymandering to achieve a forbidden racial discrimination. School officials are not operating a dual system when they fail accurately to anticipate the full effect of their racially neutral retention of a neighborhood school system, absent a finding of segregative intent. Action taken by school officials to improve racial imbalance was not an 'abandonment' of the neighborhood school system so as to preclude officials from relying on theory of neighborhood system to support position of not having violated constitutional mandates in operation of school system. The burdens, inconveniences, of integration of school system should not be placed discriminatorily."

1974: *Milliken* v. *Bradley,* 418 U.S. 717
"Segregative acts within the city alone cannot be presumed to have produced—and no factual showing was made that they did produce—an increase in the number of Negro students in the city as a whole. It is this

essential fact of predominantly Negro school population in Detroit—caused by unknown and perhaps unknowable factors such as in-migration, birth rates, economic changes, or cumulative acts of private racial fears—that accounts for the 'growing core of Negro schools' a 'core' that has grown to include virtually the entire city. *The Constitution simply does not allow federal courts to attempt to change that situation unless and until it is shown that the state, or its political subdivisions, have contributed to cause the situation to exist.* ... plaintiffs had not established sufficient grounds of discrimination or segregation based on state action to warrant the imposition of a proposed metropolitan desegregation plan."

1975: *Bradley* v. *Milliken* (Michigan), 402 F.Supp. 1096
"Practical problems with which a Board of Education is faced in attempting to achieve an acceptable racial balance without aggravating conditions producing a self-defeating exodus of middle class white and black people, tax burden imposed upon persons in the school district, and fact that requests by Board for millage increases have been rejected by the voters eight times are practicalities which not only may constitutionally be taken into account in formulating desegregation order, but which it would be irresponsible not to consider."

1975: *Buchanon* v. *Evans* (Delaware), 44 U.S. LW 3299
The Supreme Court affirmed a lower court's 1974 decision (*Evans* v. *Buchanon,* 393 F.Supp. 428) that there was an "interdistrict violation" in Delaware and that under the conditions established in the 1974 decision in Detroit (*Bradley* v. *Milliken,* 418 U.S. 717), there was sufficient evidence to warrant consideration of a desegregation plan which would involve Wilmington and its suburbs. It must be noted, however, that the court did not affirm the implementation of a cross-district plan. It simply affirmed an order requiring the preparation of such a multidistrict plan and additionally required a plan to be submitted that was limited to the civil boundaries of the city of Wilmington.

1975: *Oliver* v. *Kalamazoo Board of Education,* 508 F.2d 178
The court decided that where school segregation constitutes a constitutional violation, remedy is not only proper but necessary. Further, the court found that the "standard of *de jure* segregation of public schools is whether state and local agencies to substantial degree contributed to creation of maintenance of segregated schooling." Also, "Finding of *de jure* school segregation required showing: (1) action or inaction by public officials (2) with segregative purpose (3) which actually results in increased or continued segregation in the public schools."

1975: *Hart* v. *Community School Board of Education, New York School District No. 21,* 512 F.2d 37
"Mere racial imbalance in schools resulting from population shifts is not enough to spell segregation in the constitutional sense." Also, "Internal segregation statistics in junior high school, resulting from 'tracking' based on reading scores, were not particularly meaningful as an element in determining existence of racial discrimination in a constitutional sense."

1975: *Morales* v. *Shannon* (Texas), 516 F.2d 411
In *Morales* the court found " ... it is not a necessary ingredient to a unitary school system that all schools substantially reflect the racial balance of the school community as a whole." Additionally, it stated that "Ability groupings are not unnconstitutional per se."

1976: *U.S.* v. *Texas Educational Agency,* 532 F.2d 380

"Quotas may be used as a starting point in achieving desegregation of a segregated public school system; however, quotas are not an ironclad requirement."

1976: *Austin Independent School District* v. *United States,* 426 U.S. 952
Decision in this case restricts the use of busing as a remedy.

1976: *Evans* v. *Buchanon* (Delaware), 416 F.Supp. 328
"Fact that birth rates, or population shifts, or other factors also contribute to a degree of segregation will not relieve the state from its obligation to desegregate. It is the function of racial enrollment figures to serve as a signal to both the assigning officials and the court as to whether the system has, in fact, been desegregated or remains dual. Existence of a disparity in the racial characteristics of the school populations of a city and its suburbs is not a constitutional violation, standing alone."

1976: *Reed* v. *Rhodes* (Ohio), 422 F.Supp. 708
"In school desegregation cases, construction of quality neighborhood schools in response to overcrowded conditions plaguing many identifiable black schools could not be viewed as defense to claim of operating essentially dual system where much of school construction relied upon had effect of actually exacerbating isolation and identification of facilities by race." Also, "Local school board cannot use private discrimination to shield itself from allegation of exclusionary attendance areas."

1976: *Hills* v. *Gautreaux,* 425 U.S. 284
"The *Milliken* decision, which rejected a metropolitan area school desegregation order because there was no interdistrict violation or any significant interdistrict segregative effect, imposes no per se rule that federal courts lack authority to order corrective action beyond a municipal boundary where the violations occurred."

1976: *U.S.* v. *Board of School Commissioners of City of Indianapolis,* 541 F.2d 1211
"A school district may not contract its territory in order to avoid desegregation, nor may a city extend its boundaries in order to avoid desegregation."

1976: *Pasadena City Board of Education* v. *Nancy Anne Spangler,* 427 U.S. 424
"Where district court had adopted plan for desegregation of Pasadena school system which established a racially neutral system of student assignment, where order that there be no school with a majority of minority students had been met during the first year of the plan, where subsequent failure to meet that standard was not due to actions on the part of school officials but rather resulted from changes in demographics of residential pattern due to a normal pattern of people moving into, out of, and around the school system, district court exceeded its authority by enforcing its desegregation order so as to require annual readjustment of the attendance zones."

1977: *N.A.A.C.P.* v. *Lansing Board of Education* (Michigan), 559 F.2d 1042
"School authorities bound by constitutional mandate to desegregate cannot be permitted to dismantle a unitary school system and to reinstate a dual school system."

1977: *Dayton Board of Education* v. *Brinkman,* 97 S.Ct. 2766
"Federal courts have authority to restructure administration of school systems when constitutional violations on part of school officials are proven." Also, "The case for displacement of the local authorities by a federal court in a school desegregation case must be satisfactorily established by factual proof and justified by a reasoned statement of legal principles." And, "Dis-

parity between evidence of unconstitutionally segregative actions and the sweeping remedy decreed by the district court required supplementation of record and additional findings addressed to the scope of the remedy."

1979: *Penick* v. *Columbus Board of Education* (Ohio), 99 S.Ct. 831

"Since there is often a substantial reciprocal effect between color of school and color of neighborhood it serves, with actions of school authorities having significant impact on housing patterns, school authorities could and should act with an integrative rather than a segregative influence upon housing and should not aggravate racial imbalance in the schools by their official actions." Also, "To show segregative 'intent or purpose' in school desegregation case, plaintiffs need not prove that defendants intended to do harm or acted with ill will, but only that school officials intended to segregate, and a presumption of segregative purpose arises when plaintiffs establish that the natural, probable, and foreseeable result of public officials' action or inaction was an increase or perpetuation of the school segregation, and such presumption becomes proof unless defendants affirmatively establish that their action or inaction was a consistent and resolute application of racially neutral policies."

Appendix B:
Glossary of Terms

AFFIRMATIVE ACTION: Establishing parity with regard to race and/or sex in the assignment or employment of personnel. Operationally, it entails an overt attempt to fill vacant positions with otherwise qualified persons who are members of identifiably underrepresented groups.

ALTERNATIVE SCHOOL: A schooling experience for students unable to function in a traditional learning setting. This schooling experience is a common option in large urban schools and is not necessarily a component of school desegregation plans.

ATTENDANCE ZONE: A geographically defined area within a school district. Attendance zones prescribe the student population assigned to a specific school.

CIVIL RIGHTS COMMISSION: Federal agency that monitors and reports on discrimination and segregation in American society.

CLUSTERING: A desegregation technique involving the grouping of attendance areas, the redesignation of the grade structure of each school, and the reassignment of students within the new grouping pattern.

COMPENSATORY EDUCATION: Educational programs, augmenting regular programs, designed to correct learning deficiencies of environmental origin that have resulted from segregative practices.

CONTIGUOUS PAIRING: The realigning of the boundaries of two adjacent attendance areas into a single attendance area containing two school buildings.

DE FACTO SEGREGATION: The separation of people by race or ethnic identity. This action can have resulted from a past action not intended to discriminate (e.g., zoning), or be a practice that has grown over time through custom (e.g., real estate policies) or a state of affairs that must be accepted for practical purposes. *De facto* segregation can be contrasted with *de jure* segregation.

DE JURE SEGREGATION: The separation of people by race or ethnic identity on the basis of official legal practice or policy of a governmental body.

DESEGREGATION: The reassignment of students and staff by race or ethnic identity so that the racial identifiability of the individual school and classes within the school is removed.

EDUCATIONAL PARKS: Large school sites with several buildings, centralized administration, consolidated media, and physical education facilities. Frequently, upward of 10,000 students are served in a grade structure from pre-K to grade 12. The educational park is an organizational concept.

EMERGENCY SCHOOL ASSISTANCE ACT (ESAA): Federal legislation passed in 1972, which provides federal funds to local school districts and nonprofit organizations for programs that address educational problems resulting from the implementation of a desegregation plan.

ETHNIC: Individual identity as a result of the national origin and/or cultural characteristics of a group.

FEEDER PATTERNS: The elementary attendance areas and junior high/middle school attendance areas that comprise a high school attendance area. All students who live in a certain area will attend together the same elementary school, the same junior high/middle school, and, ultimately, the same high school.

FREEDOM OF CHOICE: Official school policy permitting a student's parents to select the school they wish their child to attend; a school system with freedom of choice will not have school attendance boundaries. Freedom of choice has not been an effective desegregation tool by itself, and desegregation plans relying substantially on freedom of choice are not likely to be approved.

GERRYMANDERING: The arbitrary and, frequently, irregular drawing of school attendance boundaries so as to include or exclude specific neighborhoods or ethnically/racially identifiable groups of students.

IN LOCO PARENTIS: The limited right of a governmental agency to act in the place of a parent.

ISLANDS: A desegregative action whereby a school is taken out of service, and the attendance area is subdivided. The students living in the subdivision are then assigned contiguously or noncontiguously to new school attendance areas.

INTEGRATION: Affirmative efforts that facilitate the elimination of racial and ethnic indifferences and at the same time provide multiethnic atmosphere and mechanisms to encourage mutual respect, understanding, and acceptance.

MAGNET SCHOOL: A school with a unique educational program or a unique organizational pattern that attracts students on a volunteer basis rather than on an assigned basis.

METROPOLITAN PLAN: A desegregation plan that crosses established school district or curl unit lines. In effect, metropolitan plans call for interdistrict remedies to segregation.

NEIGHBORHOOD SCHOOL: Colloquial term referring to a school that services, exclusively, the student who resides in the immediate proximity of the school building. This concept of school has become a rallying point for those groups who oppose school desegregation.

NONCONTIGUOUS PAIRING: The realignment of two nonadjacent attendance areas into a single attendance area with two school buildings.

OFFICE OF CIVIL RIGHTS (OCR): A unit of the Department of Health, Education, and Welfare that has the primary responsibility of administering the civil rights laws in education.

PAIRING: The realignment of two attendance areas into a single attendance area with two schools. The grade structures of each school in the paired area is then redesignated so that all students living in the paired attendance areas must attend both schools for certain years of their education.

RESEGREGATION: The return of previously desegregated schools to segregated conditions. Population mobility and the disposition of some parents to send their children to private schools are frequent causes of this.

REVERSE DISCRIMINATION: Establishing rules, policies, or laws that establish fixed quotas or that allow advantage to less qualified people simply because they belong to an identifiable racial or ethnic group.

REZONING: The redrawing of attendance area boundaries so that the newly constituted attendance areas more closely reflect the racial composition of the entire school community.

SPECIAL MASTER: An expert appointed by the court to act as the representative of the court in the development of a desegregation remedy.

VOLUNTARY DESEGREGATION: A desegregation plan in which citizens of the school community decide to desegregate their schools without direction from the courts.

WHITE FLIGHT: Refers to the tendency for white middle- and upper-class families to relocate out of communities that implement desegregation plans.

Index